THE BEST OF RED SMITH

The Best of
RED SMITH

Foreword by Tom Meany

Illustrated by Willard Mullin

J. LOWELL PRATT & COMPANY
PUBLISHERS
NEW YORK

Published by J. Lowell Pratt & Company, New York and on the
same day by The Copp Clark Company, Toronto, Canada.

The volumes in The American Sports Library are nationally distributed by The Kable News Company, New York and are represented to the booktrade by McCauley Enterprises, Box 814, Green-
wich, Conn.

Designed by The Drawing Board Inc.

FOREWORD

To say Red Smith is delightful reading for a sports fan is like saying fresh air is good for you. Red is not only a good sports writer, he is also—and which, in my opinion, is far more difficult—a good sports reporter. To write well is a talent of sorts, but to be an objective reporter requires hard work, a step removed from manual labor.

Smith did not burst full blown upon New York when he joined the Herald Tribune in late 1945. Red already was recognized as a sports authority in Milwaukee, St. Louis and Philadelphia. He possessed then, as he does now, not only the gift of writing entertainingly but also the gift of knowing his subject.

Don't be misled by the soft charm of Red's columns. When he takes off the gloves, he can slug with the best of them. Ask Albert B. (Happy) Chandler, "the greatest baseball commissioner since Judge Landis." Until Ford Frick came along, of course. Smith has a deft needle which he often employs to puncture self-inflated pomposities.

Anybody who has been a working newspaperman must respect Smith. He turns out his columns on the spot and under the gun. Red goes to no sports event with a preconceived idea of what he is to write, nor armed with frozen similies or oft-told tales to weave into his column. He lets the action itself write his column.

To read Smith, even though you've read him before, is a pleasure. If you're reading Red for the first time, I only can ask, "Where have you been?"

TOM MEANY

Brooklyn, N. Y., Nov., 1962.

Table of Contents

The Champ's Best Fight ...

Rocky Marciano

June 1954   New York

Leaving the weigh-in ceremonies, Rocky Marciano, the heavyweight champion of the world, and his court retainers hesitated just inside the windowed doors of Madison Square Garden, as though shrinking back from the crowds on the sidewalk. They chose the door closest to the auto waiting at the curb, and plunged for the car in a flying wedge formation. A burst of shouting rose in Fiftieth Street. "Hey, Rock!" "Hiya, Rocky boy!" "Yay, Champ!"

A man in the foyer listened and smiled appreciatively. "There's a sound," he said, "that will stay with him all his life."

The car with its motorcycle escort pulled away quickly but stopped for a traffic light at Eighth Avenue. Men dashed through the traffic to jam around it, shouting through the windows. Then the light changed and the machine was gone, taking Marciano to the hideout where he would loaf until time to start for Yankee Stadium and his tryst with Ezzard Charles.

Excitement lingered in the street that he had left. There was warmth in the cheering because this is a popular champion, though the heavyweight champion of the world always hears such shouts, whoever he may be, especially on a day like this. In all of sports there is no other day that holds quite the same carnival quality of excitement as the day of a heavyweight title fight.

This was a little after noon. A little earlier, the fight mob had swirled into the Garden in an unruly tide. A man caught and buffeted in the press at the door gasped as the breath was pressed out of him. "If anybody takes this much punishment in the ring, it'll be the fight of the century."

1

The Garden has had many shows that couldn't draw the house attracted by the chance to see two men in silk drawers stand on a scale. All the paid-up members of the mob were there, in the ring and around it, and in the rear stood two dark strangers in floor-length robes, lace-curtain shawls over the shoulders, embroidered yomelkas on their heads.

In the ring they were solemn as witnesses at a hanging, and, indeed, the roped platform looked not unlike a gibbet with the microphone suspended over the center by a long line like the hangman's.

"I've learned lately," said an irrelevant visitor from Boston, "that when Rocky was in high school in Brockton, Harvard wanted him as a student, majoring in football."

The man's companion was aghast. "Judas!" he said. "Imagine Rocky as an educated pauper, with muscles like his!"

Afterward, some guys walked to Dempsey's for lunch, talking about the heavyweight championship and how it sets a man apart, gives him something that nobody ever can take away. There were crowds outside Dempsey's, too, knots of strollers stopped to stare through the window at a table where the old champ sat signing autographs.

One of the guys was reminded of a breakfast with Jack in Chicago in 1949 when Charles and Walcott were out there fighting for the vacant title. This was twenty-three years after Dempsey lost the crown. A stranger stopped by that breakfast table and saluted Jack, telling him he'd seen him win the title from Jess Willard in Toledo. Jack was giving him the "Hiya, Pal" routine when the man said earnestly:

"Jack, I hope you knock the brains out of that guy tomorrow night."

He walked away and Dempsey stared after him.

"He thinks I'm still champion," Jack said softly.

When a lightning bolt carved its initials on a tree ten feet from Ezzard Charles's training quarters at Kutscher's Country Club, the former heavyweight champion of the

2

world slept the sleep of the pure in heart. Another evening when a fire broke out nearby, he lay in the deep and peaceful slumber that usually overtakes men *after* they start trading punches with Rocky Marciano, not before.

Through the tranquil Catskill nights, Ezzard floated in dreams of glory, savoring the triumph that would come to the first man on earth who could regain the heavyweight title that he had lost.

He really packed in that shut-eye, and perhaps he was "slept out," as the saying goes, when he arrived in Yankee Stadium Thursday night. That would explain why he could not be induced to doze under the most powerful anesthetic Marciano was able to supply.

However you analyze cause and effect, this was one of the great fights for the heavyweight championship. It is no disparagement of the invulnerable champion to say it was Charles who made it so.

When he was expected to retreat and cover, he fought boldly, moving in at first with right swings to the body and a left hook to the head, later countering with good right crosses. Where it had been felt he would seek safety in sticking and running, he made virtually no use of the sharp left jab he used to employ.

It had been believed that Marciano's strength would prove too great for any opponent who sought to tie him up inside, yet Charles seemed stronger than Rocky at the start, and the champion could do little at close quarters in the first few rounds.

Knocking out forty opponents in forty-five fights, Marciano had convinced virtually everybody that the man didn't live who could trade blows with him and stand through fifteen rounds. Charles traded with him. Ezzard's countenance was his receipt for the transaction. His features slowly changed, until the man who came out of the challenger's corner for the fifteenth round bore scarcely a recognizable resemblance to the one who had walked out for the first.

Yet when the final bell rang, Ezzard walked back unassisted, an unconquered loser.

If it was Ezzard's best fight, then for that very reason it

was also Rocky's best. Charles was the best man Marciano ever fought. He had better scientific equipment, at least as much courage, and a greater capacity to endure punishment than any other.

Consequently, Rocky had to make his best fight to win. Doing so, he exhibited again the two qualities for which he has been chiefly distinguished in the past—his incredible indifference to pain and the numbing force of his punch.

In addition, Marciano displayed other powers which he had never before used so ably and with such effect. He was a far more accomplished workman with short inside punches than the Marciano of earlier shows, far more accomplished in this respect than his adversary.

The point has been made before but probably will have to be made again that a man need not be a fencing master to win a decision over a boxer. One man can outscore another man by wading in, punching without respite, and whacking the whey out of the superior stylist. Rocky never let up, even when his vision was impaired by blood from a cut above his left eye.

There were times when Charles, sitting in his corner, looked as though he wanted to cry with discouragement and pain. He always came back for more, though, riding with most of Marciano's best blows, countering gamely and accurately.

It is difficult to believe there is another heavyweight extant who could give the champion so good a battle. England's Don Cockell is accused of some ability but not yet convicted. It seems strange that such targets as Nino Valdes and Hurricane Jackson should covet what Charles got. Still, it's a living, provided a guy does live.

Taking Up a Cudgel in Behalf of Saratoga

August 1954   New York

There is seldom any prodding urge in this corner to take up cudgels, hold briefs or bear fardels, partly because there is no very clear idea here of what a fardel is. However, even the most forbearing of neighbors can be goaded into protest when a small cornet player in the apartment across the court assaults "Three Coins in the Fountain" for the seventy-third time hand running.

A somewhat similar irritation is caused by incessant reiteration of the gospel that Saratoga must go because the dowager queen of American racing contributes less money than some other bridle paths toward the care and feeding of public servants. It is an old song, and unmelodious: The state is losing large sums in taxes by permitting Saratoga to operate; therefore, let's kick the crutches out from under the old girl and put on an extra shift in the salt mines of the metropolitan district.

The basis of this argument is a contention that racing has no other reason or excuse for existence than the production of money for the state treasury. It is an attitude one might expect to encounter in insatiable Albany, but it is also expressed on the same sports pages that publish racing news, presumably on the theory that racing is a sport.

Curiously, the same argument is never made regarding baseball, college football, prize fighting or curling. These are lofty and ennobling pursuits. Racing is something evil that must pay millions in tribute in order to exist in a community that abhors sin but enjoys profiting from it.

Obviously, if it is wrong for Saratoga to operate because it does not yield enough political swag, then it is a mistake to license plants away out on Long Island like Belmont, Aqueduct and Jamaica, and confine their activity to a mere seven and a half months a year.

There is room in Central Park for a track encircled by stands accommodating 150,000 spectators, where races

5

could be started at fifteen-minute intervals from 9 a.m. to midnight seven days a week, fifty-two weeks a year. The minimum betting unit should be 50 cents except for children, who would have 25 cent mutuel windows of their own. No admission charge, of course.

Disloyal citizens found loitering outside the track with money in their pockets would be beaten with bamboo flails unless they could prove they were on their way to the Polo Grounds to bet on the Giants.

Thus, and thus only, can racing justify its existence. Unless, that is, you consider racing a pleasant pastime which, in a few favored places like Saratoga, retains some trace of its early character as sport. In that event, you might feel that if Saratoga were to pass, something oddly valuable would die with it.

Casey Stengel Could Of Quit

September 1954   New York

Casey Stengel could have quit with honor after the season of 1949, his first as manager of the Yankees. Hardly anybody had expected the Yankees to win the pennant that year. They had finished third in 1948 and Bucky Harris had been fired. Physically and spiritually, the Yankees were breaking up when Casey came on from the Pacific Coast.

His first season was the year of Joe DiMaggio's hot heel, which kept Joe out of centerfield through April, May and June, and the September bout with pneumonia in which Joe lost fifteen pounds. Charley Keller played only occasionally that year, his last with the Yankees. Tommy

Henrich was still a star but as his time grew short he, too, needed relief more often than in the past.

In spite of everything, and especially in spite of the Red Sox, the Yankees did win. It was a personal triumph for the comical old cuss whom so many had put away as a clown. Not dependent on the job financially, he was in a position to exit laughing and leave 'em cheering.

"But," he has explained since then, "that first year could of been an accident." He had to stay and prove it wasn't.

His team won again in 1950 and now there was another consideration. The challenge of rebuilding the Yankees commanded his attention. Already some young fellows had made their presence felt, fellows like Gerry Coleman and Whitey Ford. There was a kid named Billy Martin sitting on the bench. There were others on the farms, and Casey knew all about them.

"They'll be here after I'm gone," he said, "and as long as they're around they'll have a little bit of old Case in 'em."

This was something he could not resist, the opportunity to work with young players and help in their development so that his mark would always be on them. Then when he did retire—and he always had a notion that day wasn't too far away—these kids would be his monument. To a man dedicated to baseball as he is, this means infinitely more than records in a book.

So for the third time the Yankees won under Stengel, and of course there was no backing off now. In all the years since Doubleday, only John McGraw and Joe McCarthy had commanded four straight pennant winners, only McCarthy's Yankees had won the world championship four times in a row. Nobody could pass up the chance to match that record.

If that was an irresistible challenge, the one offered in the spring of 1953 was even more so.

"The one biggest sports story of this year," a fellow said to him in the St. Petersburg, Fla., training base, "is Stengel and the Yankees. Can they make it five straight, as nobody ever did?"

7

"Sure," Casey said, meaning sure that was the big question, not sure he could win. "Or else I might of quit." This was the first time he'd ever voluntarily brought up the question of retiring, though he'd been asked about it often enough. He had made four passes with the dice, though, and now he had to go for broke. Everybody knew that.

"I don't know where to go for advice on how to do it," he said, speaking of the fifth straight that nobody had ever won, "but if I do it, then I can give others advice."

Of course he did it, and that was the time to quit if he was ever going to. He didn't have to go for six. Mrs. Stengel was dead set against it. Thousands who had rooted for him to get the record and rejoiced when he made it, found themselves unable to pull for the Yankees this year. If baseball was to preserve even the illusion of competition, it was high time for a change.

Chances are nobody except Casey himself knows why he persisted. He must have known how enthusiastically the whole country would receive the defeat of the Yankees, and he must have realized that if he did lose it would create a new problem with regard to retirement.

"If I quit now," he has undoubtedly told himself since the Indians won the pennant, "they'll say I couldn't take it. They'll say I just rode along while the team was winning and walked out as soon as the breaks went against me."

In the circumstances, it was hardly a stunning surprise when he signed on for next season and the year after. Everybody knew he'd be invited back. He had said he ought to be fired if the Yankees lost, and now he says he can look back and recognize mistakes he made this year, but if he thinks that is so he is the only one who does. The Yankees won more games losing the pennant than they ever did winning it for him.

If he wins next year, what then? Who would try to guess?

Happy Birthday, Grantland Rice

November 1954   New York

Since it was only Sunday evening when it began, chances are Grantland Rice's birthday party will be settling into stride about the time these pages become a shroud for some obsolete haddock. There've been some memorable wingdings in Mr. Toots Shor's fish and chips hutch, but none topped this and none ever could.

It wasn't the people present who made it the best. It was the man who was not there, though he wasn't really absent, either. What happened more than once since Grant died last July kept happening again and again Sunday night; you found yourself gazing around the merry room in absentminded questing, expecting to see Granny at the merriest table.

It was amusing to see men who live all their lives in a swarm of autograph-seekers going around this time collecting signatures from others, signatures that would fill the register of a Hall of Fame in any sport or almost any other field from show business to politics.

Yet what else would you expect? Jack Dempsey, Gene Tunney, Earl Sande, Gene Sarazen, Vinnie Richards, the Four Horsemen, Johnny Weismuller, Herman Hickman,

Lou Little, Tommy Henrich, Yogi Berra, Eddie Arcaro, Ted Atkinson, Hank Greenberg—where else would they be on a night the clan was lifting a tall one to Granny?

Wherever they were, in Miami or Nashville, Cleveland, Chicago or California, they dropped what they were doing and came on. There wasn't one among them, however famous, however successful, who doesn't owe much to Grantland Rice.

It was the biggest haul of debtors this side of Old Bailey, and they were there to pay up in the only coin Granny would ever accept—affection and laughter.

This was the party Granny's friends had been planning for several years. It didn't come off earlier because they'd never got together on a date and, anyway, there was grave doubt that Granny would have attended an affair in his honor at gunpoint. This date sort of picked itself; it was the eve of the seventy-fourth anniversary of Grant Rice's birth and the night before publication of his memoirs, "The Tumult and the Shouting."

There was nobody to sing "Happy Birthday" to, but they could have sung it loudly, for it was a happy occasion. Granny is missed but he is not mourned. There was no tear-jerking; that would have embarrassed Granny.

Rube Goldberg thought of this while watching Douglas Fairbanks Jr. on Ed Sullivan's television show. (Some of the guests went to the studio before dinner and the others watched from the party.) Fairbanks was giving a graceful reading of Granny's moving verse, "Ghosts of the Argonne":

"You can hear them at night when the moon
    is hidden;
"They sound like the rustle of winter leaves . . ."

The party was quiet. "If Granny were here now," Rube said to Col. Red Reeder, of West Point, "he'd be talking."

"Right," another said, "he'd be asking Red here, 'Hey, how about that Virginia team pretty near beating Army?' Or he'd want to know what you thought about the election, Rube. Or he'd be talking about some book he'd just read, not his."

10

Gen. Rosie O'Donnell was across the room. He and his West Point sidekick, Gen. Blondie Saunders, were two of Granny's all-time favorites. Mrs. Kit Rice tells of the morning her squire got home showing traces of wear, but full of reassurances.

"Everything's all right, honey," he said, "I've been out with Rosie and Blondie."

Everything's still all right with Granny. Nothing can be said of him now that he didn't say better of somebody else. For example, there is a verse he addressed to Charon, the boatman of the Styx, after many of his friends had died:

> "The Flame of the Inn is dim tonight—
> "Too many vacant chairs—
> "The sun has lost too much of its light—
> "Too many songs have taken flight—
> "Too many ghosts on the stairs—
> "Charon—here's to you—as man to man—
> "I wish I could pick 'em the way you can."

Jim Crow and the Color of Money

December 1954   New York

Before there were Negroes in organized baseball, Jim Crow's affairs were none of baseball's business. When the teams went South in the spring it was for physical, not social, training. If the players noticed that Negroes sat only in one section of the bleachers, or if they read the signs on the railroad stations, "Waiting Room, White," why, they accepted it as local custom that had nothing to do with them.

The visitor who mentioned the position of the Negro in the South heard a stock answer: "We know how to treat them down here and they keep their place. They're happier here than in your big cities up north with their slums and race riots."

Then Branch Rickey and Jackie Robinson broke baseball's color line. Baseball became an important area of influence in the nation's uncertain groping toward real democracy. It is no longer possible for baseball men to regard Jim Crow regulations in sports as something as remote from their affairs as voodoo drums in Haiti. Whether they like it or not, baseball men now must set an example in interracial relations.

That is why the Yankees should not knuckle down to Birmingham's Jim Crow baseball ordinance and play an exhibition game in the Alabama city next spring. Because of their pre-eminence in the game, the Yankees should be the last to conform to any local segregation policy.

Up to last year, Birmingham forbade "mixed" sports events involving Negro and white participants. Then the ordinance was repealed, and both the Dodgers and Giants played exhibitions there last spring. The Dodgers' weekend game drew well, the Giants and Indians only moderately in mid-week, Negroes making up a large majority of the crowds.

Since then, through a referendum in which balloting

was very light, Birmingham restored the ban on mixed sports. The Dodgers are by-passing the town on their spring tour. So are the Giants, at a substantial financial sacrifice, for this is Willie Mays' home and Willie, playing with the world champions, could fill the park.

Chances are the crowd that would pay to see Willie and the other Giants would be mostly Negro, too, but the pigmentation of a fan's skin doesn't affect the color of his money. The Dodgers or the Giants and their Cleveland traveling companions couldn't give a bona fide exhibition without using their Negro players. The Yankees can, and have scheduled a game there.

Elston Howard, a catcher-outfielder, is the only Negro expected to report to the Yankee training camp. He has not yet made the team and perhaps he may not make it, though his chances are highly regarded in the Yankee office. Whether he makes it or not, he won't be used in Birmingham.

Jackie Robinson, barnstorming with a Negro team that included several white players, ran afoul of the Birmingham ordinance a couple of years ago. In this instance, "no mixed sports" meant "no whites allowed," and although at first blush it might seem ludicrous to consider this racial discrimination, it wasn't ludicrous at all because it was merely a reverse application of the same abhorrent principle.

A Negro newspaper in Birmingham called upon Robinson to resist. Editorially, it urged him to defy the ordinance and thus test its validity, or else cancel the game. Instead he knuckled down as the Yankees mean to knuckle down.

Robinson explained that he hadn't booked the tour but was merely lending his name and services to the organization, playing wherever the booking office scheduled a game. It was a mistake on his part:

Robinson is keenly and properly conscious of his importance in the Negro's struggle for recognition. Here was an opportunity to dramatize the cause in far more sympathetic circumstances than Jackie has encountered on other occasions. He blew the chance.

Even if he wins a job as a regular, there will be times

13

in the spring when Elston Howard won't play, in order
that he may have a day off or so Casey Stengel can try
out another candidate. There is no reason why he
shouldn't get his day off in St. Petersburg or Miami or
Birmingham—except that in Birmingham it's a matter of
yielding to pressure.

The Yankees could play Howard and make a test case
of the ordinance's dubious legal standing. That would be
an uncharacteristic bit of crusading, though. The Yankees
have the Southern Association farm in Birmingham. They
have no special wish to alienate any of the population
through a political-social dispute.

They don't have to carry a torch, but they do their
credit no good by giving aid and comfort to the voodoo
worshippers. They could stay out of Birmingham—except
that a crowd of 15,000 there would represent a nice
financial touch for their local affiliate. Curious how often
that consideration bobs up.

Football Code: Guile's Good, Deceit's Dastardly

October 1955   New York

The football season was half over before one college
coach publicly accused another of malpractice, misfeasance, halitosis and conduct unbecoming an opponent.
This could mean that brother love is on the upswing and
the world is becoming a happier place to live in, with or
without bunged knees, cleat-scarred features and similar
marks of the man of culture. It used to be that the
coachly clan couldn't get through two warm-up games
before spitballs were being thrown.

This week the haunting wail of the loser is heard
around Gainesville, Fla., where Bob Woodruff, molder of
youth at the University of Florida, has raised a cry of
dirty pool against Blanton Collier, architect of character
at Kentucky.

Woodruff says a Kentucky guard faked an injury and stopped the clock thirty-four seconds before the end of the Kentucky-Florida game last Saturday. This enabled Collier to change quarterbacks without penalty, and the new man kicked a field goal that won the game, 10 to 7.

Collier says this is a low canard in the first place, and in the second no gent would go around spreading stories like that without first inviting his adversary to put up his hands. Under the code, the honorable rattlesnake gives warning before a strike.

The Associated Press quotes Woodruff: "There is considerable evidence Kentucky coaches may have been responsible for a dishonest, unsportsmanlike and deceitful act that produced Kentucky's winning field goal."

"I deny that I have ever coached or instructed any player to fake an injury," Collier retorts. "Woodruff was wrong in making such a statement. Out of fairness to me, he should have contacted me first."

Watch your language, gentlemen, there are football players present.

It will, of course, be recalled that in the closing seconds of a game with Iowa two years ago a Notre Dame lineman stopped the clock by falling into a melodramatic swoon. The time thus gained was employed by Notre Dame to tie the score, 14 to 14.

Because Notre Dame was involved and Notre Dame is always in the spotlight, this created a national crisis and the government teetered perilously. There was agitation for a rule forbidding fakery, though it was not clear how an official could enforce same without a lie detector. Ultimately the lawgivers put the points of their heads together and promulgated the doctrine that to tell or act a lie was untruthful.

A sounder suggestion was made by a former college president, but he put it forward privately, not for publication, and there is a possibility that he wasn't entirely serious. He proposed that before a game the players of each team draw up in ranks along the sideline, lift their right hands and solemnly pledge not to deceive or attempt to deceive anybody. This would, of course, outlaw the buck-lateral sequence.

Whenever time is running out in a close game, a glorious inconsistency creeps into football thinking. There are assorted dodges for stopping the clock—taking the ball out of bounds when it can't be advanced, for example—and they are warmly approved.

There are also devices for keeping the clock running. It is common to see the team that is in front freeze the ball in the last few minutes, deliberately taking too much time in the huddle and accepting penalties for it, stodgily running one play after another into the line while time drains away. This is applauded as sound strategy.

It seems here that the only difference between stopping the clock and speeding it up is a difference of expedience. The only reason why it is evil to fake an injury is that this involves deceit, though guile is a commodity highly admired in football. If players are required to preserve themselves in the best possible health through the last two minutes, then they should also be expected to run their plays as rapidly as possible so the other team may have another chance.

Somewhere in the football coaches' code there is a prohibition against speaking ill of one another. The theory is that they all have to live in one nest and none of them should foul it.

A coach is hired to teach boys to play the game as well as they are able, but only in certain circumstances. Once his team has made victory safe, then he's supposed to send in his least talented substitutes, restrict their repertoire of plays, order them to punt on first down, somehow insure that they play as poorly as they are able so the losing coach won't be disgraced by a lopsided score.

Even if one is guilty of dishonest, unsportsmanlike, deceitful behavior, nobody's supposed to blow the whistle. If he gets that kind of reputation, how'll he ever make a buck as a builder of men?

O'Malley's House of Horrors

December 1955   New York

Walter O'Malley, president of the world champion Dodgers of Jersey City, shares with other persuasive men a gift for supporting an argument with figures that can't easily be checked. James Thurber, when he wishes to smash an adversary in debate, employs a similar tactic. "As you know, of course," he says, "the Prestwick Report settles all doubts on that score," etc. The other fellow has not read the Prestwick Report, partly because there is no such thing, backs off in mortified surrender, ashamed of his ignorance.

John McNulty, passing without credentials through a gate at the racetrack attended by a Pinkerton who does not know him, merely jerks a thumb toward the man behind him in line and says, "He's all right, he's with me." If you are vouching for another, it stands to reason that you're all you pretend to be and probably more.

Back to O'Malley. He has said more than once that physical maintenance of Ebbets Field cost $100,000 a year. When he first proposed moving some of Brooklyn's home games to Jersey City, a question was raised about the expense of restoring a ball park that had been abandoned for years to mosquitoes and automobile races. O'Malley said pooh, it could be done for $25,000.

While amateur mathematicians were pondering these figures—$25,000 to convert a racing plant into a ball park and $100,000 to maintain a ball park as a ball park—Jersey authorities came up with an estimate of $129,-000 for the refurbishing job. Is it still Mr. O'Malley's plan, as he said in the beginning, to pay for the reconditioning plus $10,000 rental? That seems to add up to an investment of $139,000 for seven games in a park that holds 10,000 fewer customers than Ebbets Field.

After attending the Abbey Theater in Dublin, Roger Bannister, the foot-racer, wrote: "I asked myself why

17

every Irish phrase has a link with the heavens. Why did even their pennies bear harps?" No other Irishman excels Walter O'Malley at musical keening, at crying with a loaf of bread under each arm.

Almost every season, it is the gate for the last game that enables the Dodgers to break even. They'd have finished in the red if the World Series hadn't gone seven games. Yet over the last ten years, the Dodgers have done more business at home and on the road than any other club in the National League. How do the others manage to get by?

In the last three seasons, of course, Milwaukee attendance has offered a phenomenon unmatched in baseball. The Boston-Milwaukee total over a decade, however, doesn't touch Brooklyn's figures for the same period.

Moreover, the Dodgers own their park. For one lacking the president's acknowledged financial acumen, it is difficult to understand how he expects to increase his net by paying rent in a smaller playground, while maintenance costs continue at home . . .

In his campaign to persuade Brooklyn fans that Ebbets Field is a house of horrors which they should not visit, O'Malley has declared repeatedly that the Dodgers can't play there after 1957. Why not? They own the joint. Nobody's foreclosing.

If an ideal site were available in Brooklyn, could the Dodgers assume the huge expense of building a new stadium? Authorities have not encouraged a belief that the city would build them a new store. What's with O'Malley, then? Does he have his eye on some distant city?

If he were to propose moving now to Minneapolis or Los Angeles, the other owners would surely say: "Abandon the second-best corner in the league? Look, up to now we've moved only the dead horses. Act your age, Walter."

A couple of years hence, however, after constant re-iteration of Dodger woes dramatized by such devices as the Jersey City caper, the owners might come to accept the theory that Brooklyn is a ghost borough, and a change of venue might be approved.

18

There is no pretense here of ability to read a mind as deep as Mr. O'Malley's. Bannister had an encounter with the Irish grasp of finance when he sought to tip a Dublin porter for carrying his bag.

"Sure," the man scoffed, "and what would I be doing charging a handsome fellow like yourself, and you with all the Olympic glory of Zeus, and the gods of Ancient Greece, on your jacket? If I were to charge you, and heaven forbid that I should, 'twould be only three pence. Why don't you make it a shilling?"

Golf is a Gentleman's Game

December 1955   New York

Golf is a gentleman's game. This is stated without fear of contradiction, on the unimpeachable authority of the gentlemen themselves. They keep repeating it, to remind themselves. It's supposed to have the same effect as a schoolboy's assignment to write, "I must not bust teacher in the eye with a spitball," a hundred times.

In a sport whose practitioners are known to exude honor, breeding, manners and taste from every pore, it caused some commotion when Gentleman Tommy Bolt, a professional true-penny, publicly implied that his esteemed colleague, Gentleman Sam Snead, had been the beneficiary of practices abhorrent to the code of the clan. It seemed an almost ungentlemanly remark.

Mr. Bolt was "reasonably sure," he told the press, that when Mr. Snead swung the short irons, his ever-loving gallery was not content to let the chips fall where they might. He couldn't mention any specific time or place where a spectator had moved Mr. Snead's ball to improve the lie, he couldn't quote any witness to such an act, but he had talked to "thousands of people" who said this had been done.

To suggest that this bordered on gossip-mongering would be an implication that Mr. Bolt lacked the dignified reticence of a perfect gent. To mention that he was a loser lately defeated by Mr. Snead in the Miami Open would lend little to his delineation of Chesterfieldian grace.

As a class, the golfer doth protest too much, anyhow. He's interminably and everlastingly yacking about the gentleman's game, as though a mucker were instantly ennobled by the act of pulling a No. 2 wood from his bag.

The fact is, there are golfers who are vile mathematicians and can't count for sour apples. There are shuffling, unwary walkers who wouldn't dream of kicking a ball out of the rough, except by accident. There are myopic players who can't see all the way down to a clubhead grounded in the sand. The divine right of any golfer to concede himself all putts under twelve feet is honorably established, and if a man happens to sneeze while announcing his handicap, so it sounds like thirteen instead of three, he can hardly be blamed for his head cold.

In short, some players cheat. Not many years ago, a P.G.A. committee deemed it necessary to have a heart-to-heart chat with one of the members and point out that the rules didn't require his wife to precede him around the course. The committee delicately refrained from accusing her of booting her husband's ball from woods to fairway.

For many years, Sam Snead has had a passionately devoted following. In a big tournament, the gallery watching his match may line the fairway from tee to green, making it difficult for a shot to veer off course. In their enthusiasm, his idolators may trample the opponent to jelly, but if any of them deliberately improves Sam's position there is no ground for implying collusion on his part.

Mr. Bolt, expiating on what he conceived to be Mr. Snead's unaccountably good fortune in money matches, said that Sam's ball was found in a surprisingly favorable position after what looked like a wild tee shot in the Miami Open. He admitted, however, that he hadn't actually seen where the ball landed and had no evidence that it had been moved after coming to rest.

Mr. Snead said he found it in a stinking lie and was lucky to bring off a splendid recovery, slicing it toward the green around a copse of trees.

"If anybody kicked it," Sam said, entering what seems a valid complaint, "he should have kicked it a little farther."

If there's kicking to be done around here, Sam's golf ball isn't necessarily the only target available.

1/11th of the Dodger Bus. Mgr.

February 1956   New York

On Dec. 9, Irving Rudd became one-eleventh of the business manager of the Brooklyn Dodgers, which illustrates the virulence of the Casey Stengel platoon system that has spread through baseball like the bubonic plague. The Dodgers already had on their rosters men like Sandy Amoros and Junior Gilliam designated as one-third of a leftfielder, one-half of a second baseman, and so on. Arranging to play one-eleventh of their home games in Jersey City this year, they appointed Mr. Rudd the fractional business manager of that operation.

On Dec. 12 he opened one-eleventh of an office in the Plaza Hotel on Jersey City's Journal Square and invited mail orders for tickets. Since then mail has been received in gratifying quantities, but also there have come telephone calls and personal visits by various species of fauna native to the meadows across the Hudson.

First time the phone rang, it was answered briskly, not to say eagerly: "Hello, Brooklyn Dodgers."

There was an uncertain pause. Then a voice said: "Brooklyn Dodgers? Hell, I want a plane to Alaska."

Seems that Swarthmore 5-3100, a rather tony and Quakerish exchange for Brooklyn's Bums, is similar to the phone number of an air line dealing in coach flights to far places. In the last six weeks Mr. Rudd has advised many strangers regarding air travel to Guadalajara, Andorra and Miami Beach.

Most of the visitors who have walked in off the street have shown both a keen enthusiasm for baseball and familiarity with the architecture of the ball park, even though the playground has been abandoned to automobile races since the International League franchise atrophied in Jersey City some years ago. Ninety per cent of the applicants demand seats in one of two locations.

They want Section 3, which is near first base, or else they insist on seats next to Mayor Bernard J. Berry's box. In any ball park, of course, a seat near first base commands a fine view of the game. In any city, a seat next to the Mayor may furnish an opportunity to brace His Honor for a job in street cleaning or sewage disposal.

Old residents of Jersey City no doubt remember the days of Mayor Frank Hague, when any citizen who declined to buy tickets for the International League's opening game was looked upon as a mass murderer unfit to feed at the public trough. Every spring that game was sold out two or three times over, and perhaps it is still deemed advisable to be seen by the Mayor giving loyal support to the home team.

There have, however, been a few exceptions. One lady wanted seats behind the goal posts. Another offered to buy a pair of tickets provided Mr. Rudd would explain baseball to her. He recited the infield fly rule and took her money.

Afterwards is Too Late

February 1956   New York

It was, no doubt, pure coincidence that at the very hour when presses were rolling off the story about the city building a new store for Walter O'Malley, Gov. Averell Harriman and Mayor Robert Wagner were hoping aloud that the Dodgers would remain in Brooklyn and a couple of "actors" in the baseball writers' show were "singing" about the "oldest established permanent floating franchise in New York."

Some months ago, doctors took a cursory glance at the plan for a stadium at Brooklyn's hub and pronounced it dead. All of a sudden it has come to life with the joint announcement by the Mayor and John Cashmore, Brooklyn's Borough President, of a bill to enable the city to create space for a ball park.

Providing a setting suitable to the skills of Duke Snider isn't the primary objective of the measure to be introduced in Albany, nor is it necessarily an indispensable part. Rather, the plan is for a major rehabilitation project which could make room for a municipal stadium, but wouldn't have to.

The impression grows that Walter O'Malley, by dint of his dramatic venture into Jersey City and by arguing his case at every conceivable opportunity and getting himself photographed with models of super-duper Plexiglass-roofed playgrounds, has made substantial gains.

One would be tempted to describe The O'Malley as the Humbert Fugazy of baseball, except that the celebrated entrepreneur of the '20s built all his sporting palaces in his imagination, whereas the Dodgers' president may one day pour concrete.

Still, they have something of the same flair. The tale is told that Fugazy, having made innumerable official announcements of his intention of building assorted coliseums which would dwarf the Taj Mahal, arrived at last at a point where nobody was going to listen unless he could show something in the nature of an architect's sketch.

Somewhere he got hold of a picture of the state capitol of Nebraska, distributed copies, and half the papers in town published them.

Up to now, Walter O'Malley has merely insisted that the Dodgers must get out of Ebbets Field, and has been making googoo eyes at the corner of Atlantic and Flatbush avenues. It is, undeniably, a desirable site for a stadium, for here all three subway lines, all automobile traffic across the Brooklyn and Manhattan bridges, the trolley lines and the Long Island Rail Road converge.

Chances are some objections are inevitable when any proposal is made for the use of public funds to build a showcase for a privately-owned, profit-making enterprise like a baseball team. The objections are not unanswerable, however.

In the first place, most of the great cities of the world recognize the desirability of having adequate arenas for sports and other spectacles. New York is the largest city in the world that doesn't have a big public playground of its own, which is one reason it is far down the list of good football towns.

In the second place, the primary object is not to build a store for O'Malley, but to furnish the City of New York with a needed facility, for which there happens to be a tenant available to help pay the bills. There is, of course, plenty of precedent for this in Baltimore, Kansas City, Milwaukee, Cleveland and elsewhere.

Thirdly, a major league baseball team is a real asset to any city and this fact isn't altered if its proprietor happens to make a profit. There are no public improvements of any sort which don't benefit some individuals more than others, but that is no reason for not improving.

In Brooklyn, O'Malley has been operating on the second-best corner in the National League. Before Milwaukee got into the act, he had the best corner. It is difficult to believe that he could seriously entertain the idea of moving, yet Boston and Philadelphia have suffered rude shocks, and St. Louis believed Bill Veeck when he said he meant to keep the Browns there.

If a city or borough deems it important to keep a ball club at home, it is imperative to take steps before the franchise has moved. Afterward is too late.

Eddie Murphy, who wrote baseball for the old "Sun," is author of the observation that Brooklyn is the biggest town in the world without a daily newspaper, without a railroad station and without a leftfielder. If O'Malley cuts up the old Ebbets acres for honeymoon cottages, there won't even be a leftfield.

24

A Votre Wes Santee

The unfrocking of Wes Santee by the Amateur Athletic Union has exercised the suntanned press of this area at least as violently as it has aroused lawgivers in Washington, farmers in Kansas and members of the Eighth Ave. country club set in Stillman's gym. It seems generally agreed that the A.A.U. has mishandled the case with a bumbling, ponderous ineptitude unmatched this side of Puerto Rico where, Conn McCreary reports, there is a jockey who boasts with pardonable pride that he has been ruled off for life thirteen times.

Santee is a highly personable young man whom the A.A.U. has subjected to continued public embarrassment by unnecessarily dragging out the inquiries into his expense accounts, first suspending him on charges of professionalism, then reinstating him, then reversing the reversal and expelling him forever from the company of the pure and unsalaried.

There is wide sympathy for Santee personally because it appears that honesty was his unforgivable sin; if he had not given an accurate accounting of expense monies received from assorted promoters of track meets, he might never have been accused of accepting excessive payments.

In this year of Olympic foreboding, disqualification of America's fastest mile runner from amateur competition is deemed especially untimely; patrioteers feel that the A.A.U. has made the United States look utterly ridiculous in foreign eyes.

Above all, the editorial thunderers of the sports pages are shaken by what they consider a threat to one of the most sacred of American institutions—the swindle sheet.

How, they are demanding in voices lifted to catch the attention of their publishers, can the A.A.U. expect the meanest of God's creatures—to say nothing of an athlete, gentleman and officer of the Marine Corps—to live

25

and travel on a niggardly pittance of $15 a day? Is that ivory tower hermetically sealed and sound-proofed so the high priests of amateurism have never heard of inflation?

Nothing so inspires editorial eloquence, so stirs literary imagination, as a discussion of expense accounts, especially a discussion that promises to catch the attention of the boss. This is particularly true down here, where a room commanding a view of Biscayne Bay costs $26 a day and the price goes to $31 if the desk clerk smiles.

Even sports writers, a breed of monkish and ascetic tastes who are known to keep the financial interests of their employers always uppermost in their minds, require an allowance several times greater than the A.A.U.'s per diem limit to cover such bare necessities as stone crabs at Joe's on the Beach, steaks at Black Caesar's Forge and a modest excursion to Nassau for bone fishing.

The situation is not, of course, peculiar to this region. It never was. Years ago an assignment in the Far North led Gene Fowler to compose an expense account that has survived in American newspaper literature as "Hamlet" has endured in English letters.

Even in the frozen wastelands, Mr. Fowler discovered, the cost of inside straights and anti-freeze compound can be prohibitive. Though never an unimaginative man, he found, upon attempting an accounting, that the first draft of his expense sheet left him short of his goal by several hundred dollars.

Pouring himself three fingers of truth serum, he tried again. This time he included a substantial rental for a dog team and sledge, which anybody knows are indispensable to a reporter in the frostbite belt. Even that was insufficient for his needs. Sadly he added a notation that the lead dog had succumbed to the rigors of the journey, and he listed an item of $100 recompense for the noble beast's owner. Still having failed to cross over to the alkaline side, he dashed off the line that will live forever:

"Flowers for bereaved bitch, $50."

Sunshine Forever—for Granny

The Sunshine Park that Grantland Rice knew was a Shoeless Joe among racetracks, a sort of slum-clearance project in a rattlesnake colony. The barns were sagging shanties of scrap lumber, the clubhouse and grandstand featured peeling paint, and there was a seedy, carpet-slippers informality that captivated Granny. The club-house dining room was bare, plain and tiny, but it served the superlative Stevens victuals, and immediately outside were the remaining necessities of life—an open-air bar and a mutuel battery maybe fifteen feet apart and not more than six paces removed from a view of the running strip.

There were horses but hardly any people, which is not good for management but wonderful for the clientele. Granny made no secret of his affection for the place.

"Mr. Rice," asked a bright young native son interviewing him in California, "what's your favorite racetrack? Santa Anita? Hollywood? Del Mar?"

"Sunshine Park," Granny said. The startled reporter never had heard of Sunshine and was not hugely gratified when Granny described its location about the middle of a triangle made by Tampa, St. Petersburg and Clearwater.

"Well, sir," the young man inquired, trying again, "what's your favorite city? For climate, I mean."

It happened to be a miserable winter of cold and smog in Los Angeles.

"Quebec," Granny said. "You go there for snow, you get it."

Aided by Granny's benedictions, Sunshine prospered modestly, and after Granny died it got a face-lift and hair-do, with fresh paint and glassed-in restaurant on the third level, elevator and so on.

"I'm not quite sure Granny would like it," the secretary, Milo Vega, confessed dubiously, "but it's progress."

More or less as a peace offering for scrubbing up the playground which Granny had regarded with something like a parent's feeling for a small, soiled child, Sunshine inaugurated with this year's meeting a Grantland Rice Memorial Handicap and also endowed two scholarships for senior journalism students at the University of Florida and Florida State.

Saturday saw the race's first running, with nine horses of three years and older going a mile and a sixteenth for $3,500, the richest purse Sunshine has got up yet. There were, of course, some garden-variety horseplayers present, but at a casual glance it looked as though admission was by invitation on this day, for wherever you looked you saw Granny's mob.

George Weiss, the general manager of the Yankees, had a luncheon party for the baseball writers covering the St. Petersburg camp and their wives; Everett and Petey Clay flew up from Hialeah; there were special friends of Granny like Dan and Norma Parker and Frank and Lillian Graham.

Sunshine has been having an uncommonly formful meeting with the program selector picking four or five winners a day and something like 37 per cent of the favorites winning, but this day it was almost as though the results had been arranged for Granny, who doted on long shots. One after another, the outsiders came banging down to pay $47 or $55.

"Do you suppose," somebody asked, "that Granny's got a hand in this somehow?"

Stabbing through the early races, hunch-players kept groping for a good thing for Granny's race. There was a tip out on Belldiver, and that was all right because Belldiver is a six-year-old son of Devil Diver, a horse that Granny admired when his friend John Gaver was training him for his friend, Jock Whitney. The favorite at 2 to 1 in the morning line was a five-year-old gelding named Steppin Pappy. Nothing wrong with that for a hunch, either, considering how Granny was still stepping along at the top of his stride right down to the day when he collapsed at his typewriter.

"Me, though," a fellow said, "I like The Butcher, because if you ever pounded this asphalt here with Granny through nine races in the afternoon and then tried to keep up with him that night at the dog races, you know he could kill you."

Thus they joked through the balmy afternoon, who had to laugh lest they cry. They prowled the grounds, pausing at the bar to lift one in memory, strolling away up to the head of the stretch where the jockeys came whipping and war-whooping around the last turn.

Except for a few children playing in the dusty grass, and a few mothers watching them from parked cars, it was a place of deserted quiet up there. One little girl wearing patent leather Mary-Anns had climbed a cyclone fence beside the parking lot and her mother was telling her to get down lest she scuff her new shoes. Two men wearing neckties walked past and the mother said, "Here comes the president. He'll knock you down." The little one paid no attention.

In Granny's race a gray named Blue Ember, turned almost white in his sixth year, led for about three-quarters, but then the favorite, Steppin Pappy, took over and won. His trainer, K. J. Heisey, was excited in the winner's circle accepting the trophy, a handsome silver bowl with one of the finest pictures Granny ever had taken reproduced in the metal by some photographic process.

It was a simple and dignified little ceremony which Granny wouldn't have watched. He loathed winning favorites. He'd have been back at Scott Miller's mutuel window bucking for a good thing in the next race.

Off and Running, Mr. Vanderbilt

April 1956   New York

The greater gambling season of the Greater New York Association Without a Comma Inc. opened yesterday on the faded parade ground of the Jamaica horse yard amid scenes of practically indescribable splendor—indescribable, that is, in a family newspaper. At 12:45 p.m. the band played a ditty having to do with "the home of the brave," and 40,492 freemen who had not cashed a mutuel ticket in New York since Nov. 14 stood and prepared to deliver for the next 196 weekdays. It was a genuinely moving spectacle.

This was the start of the first full season under direction of the new, non-profit, super-government of New York racing which was organized last year to create a "dream track" for Metropolitan stabbers. The site chosen for the grand opening was appropriate, for under a cold gray sky Jamaica's barren meadows looked like a prairie dog's dream.

In its palmiest days as the Metropolitan Jockey Club under the presidency of John Morris—it was known variously then as Honest John's or the Morris Plan—the old cavalry post was never lovelier. The decorating motif was a sedate and dignified currency-green, with no garish flowerbeds or flamboyant flamingoes to strike a discordant note.

Necks turtled into the upturned collars of topcoats, the clientele quailed under the wind's lash. Remnants of old, second-hand snow lay in soiled drifts inside the hedge which beautifies the soggy infield. The hedge itself, unkindly used by winter, wore the defeated appearance of last year's toothbrush.

After five races, not a favorite had showed in the money. Income tax deadline was only fourteen days away.

The first beaten favorite of the new season was an entry, eight-year-old Ham Bone and four-year-old Copper Disc, which finished nowhere in the opening event behind the second choice, C. O. Dorsett. Paying $7.90, the winner set up a daily double that returned $132.30 when Sheila's Son won the second heat.

At this point, Alfred Vanderbilt made reconnaissance under the stands, and returned with a report.

"The losers," he said, "are tearing up tickets and saying, 'Who was the louse told me to bet the four horse?' The winners are shivering in front of the cashiers' windows saying, 'I'd like to find the crumb that said it would be 60 degrees or warmer today.'

"The season," Mr. Vanderbilt summed up, "is off and running. Even the winners are complaining."

30

The Unvarnished Lie

"The Harder They Fall" is being advertised as the movie "they tried to suppress because it tells the naked truth about boxing." It is a fictional version of Budd Schulberg's old novel about Primo Carnera, a fabrication based more or less on something that happened twenty-five years ago, updated to the television era to create the impression that it is happening right now. That is a Hollywood definition of unvarnished truth.

As for "their" efforts to prevent an expose, it is true that Truman Gibson, of the International Boxing Club, refused the studio permission to make crowd shots at the Rocky Marciano-Archie Moore fight last fall because he realized the movie would smear boxing. As Hollywood employs the mother tongue, this constitutes a campaign to suppress the truth.

If there is anybody who, having read the advertisements, couldn't describe the picture accurately sight unseen, then he must have been living in a cave since invention of the magic lantern.

It is a celluloid chamber of horrors housing the dustiest museum pieces of cinema—punch-drunk fighters, calloused and scheming managers, venal newspaper men, sinister racketeers. Tossed on the market now while the papers are full of investigations into boxing, this dismal charade stands to make more money than poor old Carnera earned for the mob that used him.

In one respect, the film excels several of its predecessors. It is as heavy-footed as most earlier treatments of this hackneyed theme, as faithful as any to the outworn cliche, but it touches a height of tastelessness which may not have been achieved previously.

Special credit for this accomplishment belongs to Max Baer, though the contributions of Jersey Joe Walcott and Pat Comiskey should not be overlooked. All three are former boxers, impersonating actors in this exhibit, and

two of them held the heavyweight championship. Whatever they have and are today they owe to the business
which they help traduce here.

When Ernie Schaaf died after a bout with Carnera,
his death was attributed to injuries suffered in an earlier
match with Baer. A parallel case is depicted in the film,
with Baer playing the role of the man who does the
fatal damage and subsequently boasts about it. If this is
difficult to believe, it is not unique in that respect.

However, Baer makes another and somewhat different
contribution. He appears in the ring as Buddy Brannen,
heavyweight champion of the world. You need only one
glance at his waistline to be reassured that this is, after
all, strictly fiction.

Over the years Hollywood keeps learning new tricks
with the magic lantern, keeps making technical advances.
Though there is no evidence here that the script writers
have kept pace, this is probably the best fight film,
photographically, made to date. The ring action is excel-
lent, even when it exaggerates the ineptitude of the goon
representing Carnera.

Hollywood does not, of course, mention Carnera or
admit that he was the prototype of Toro Morena, a simple
bewildered Argentine giant played with fine sympathy by
Mike Lane. Chances are, therefore, it is idle to object
that even old Primo was a better fighter than this un-
believable tiger of the screen, whose aging trainer can
stiffen him with one bare-handed swat.

As the underworld boss who imports this great, harm-
less booby and exploits him, Rod Steiger is first-rate.
There isn't a more convincing sinister influence in Hollywood's entire line of stock models. Humphrey Bogart,
billed as the star, just goes over the course for exercise
this time. One has the impression that he read the script,
said, "That old thing," and walked through it.

As a cynical ex-newspaper man turned press agent, he
manages to keep his essential nobility under wraps for
105 minutes of running time. When at long last his
abused conscience asserts itself he slides a single sheet
of paper into a typewriter—not two sheets, like a newspaper man—and spells out the message:

"The boxing business must rid itself of the evil influence of racketeers and crooked managers—even if it takes an act of Congress to do it."

It is a bold stroke. Bring on some more sinners.

An Award to Mr. Fitz

April 1956   New York

Within reach of the typewriter that is mispelling these words hangs an autographed portrait of James E. Fitzsimmons. It is the only formal photograph the great trainer ever sat for, and it is a triumph—Sunday suit brushed and pressed and buttoned, stop-watch on wrist, unwrinkled bow tie on the triumphantly laundered shirt.

Mr. Fitz seems to be getting mischievous amusement out of the business of posing. There's just the beginning of a smile on his lips; there's a wonderful twinkle in the young, direct eyes; a monument of character is there, kindly, forthright, wise and humorous.

"After eighty years," he could be thinking, "they bring me down here and set me in front of velvet drapes and tell me to watch the birdie. All those hard years and good ones, all those winners and losers, all those snapshots in the winner's circle and all those times I couldn't get there—like the day the state trooper ran me off after Gallant Fox had won the Derby. And now this. Well, it's a great life."

When the photograph was delivered, Mr. Fitz kind of

liked it. He studied it with a little, self-disparaging grin. When he spoke it was an old jockey talking.

"That time," he said, "I was really trying."

On Thursday of this week Mr. Fitz will have to put on the Sunday suit again. He is to be guest of honor at a luncheon in the Waldorf where he will receive the annual award for outstanding sportsmanship from the Sportsmanship Brotherhood.

The Brotherhood is an organization with a single purpose, perhaps a sentimental one. It exists only to help keep sportsmanship alive in sports, to preserve some meaning in the word in an age when sentimental labels are widely regarded as "square." It doesn't command much space on the sports pages. Amateurs who take money under the table and fighters who take to the water make livelier news.

There never have been any foolish provisions restricting the honor to amateurs. The men who created the Brotherhood saw their purpose straight and had the sense to realize that an honest living honestly earned does not disqualify a sportsman. The first recipient was a professional—Walter Johnson in 1927—and there have been many since: Lou Gehrig and Connie Mack and Mel Ott and Billy Southworth; Willie Hoppe and Ben Hogan and Fielding Yost and A. A. Stagg.

Over the years, however, the award never has gone to a man on the racetrack, though the committee was crowding right up against the rail in 1939 when it chose Grantland Rice, the patron saint of the daily double. Mr. Fitz is the first who made the horses pay him.

When Gustavus T. Kirby, the elder statesman of amateur sport, died a month ago, Dan Chase, executive director of the Brotherhood, attended the funeral in Mount Kisco. So did many members of the Amateur Athletic Union brass, and afterward some of Gus' special friends gathered in the old Kirby homestead where Wilhelmina Kirby Waller lives with her horse-training husband, Tom Waller.

Chase happened to mention the selection of Mr. Fitz for the sportsmanship award, startling one exhibit in the A.A.U. waxworks, who may have been thinking of something like the A.A.U.'s Sullivan Award for amateurs.

"Why," this guy asked, "would they pick a professional? And a man from the racetrack, especially?"

Mrs. Waller took a full wind-up.

"I'll tell you why," she said. "In a business that is loaded with temptations to be crooked, Mr. Fitz has been absolutely straight for eighty years. That's the reason."

"You," Tom Waller told his wife, "can say that again."

Fact is, of course, anything you say about Mr. Fitz you can say again and again. You can, and the boys do, whenever they talk about him or write about him. Of the many simple pleasures in life, none is greater than to have an hour with that gentleman and just listen to his tales.

You get the impression that he hasn't forgotten anything since the day Grover Cleveland was inaugurated as President, which was also the day young Jim Fitzsimmons got a job galloping horses at Sheepshead Bay.

Most people, even old horse players, have forgotten that there ever were tracks named St. Asaph, or Alexander Island, or Gloucester, or that place near the Patapsco River in Maryland where they had tomatoes growing in the infield. Mr. Fitz hasn't forgotten, though, because he was there.

Of course, just living eighty-one years and getting around a good deal doesn't necessarily call for hosannahs. There are other reasons for honoring Mr. Fitz, and Joe Palmer stated a big one rather aptly. "Mr. Fitz," Joe wrote, "deserves a silver plate just for being him."

Pity the Poor Umpire . . .
Drs. Frisch and duRocher

April 1956   New York

This is a sort of "get well" message to one Patrick Badden, a supervisor of umpires for the National Baseball Association. Under a headline announcing, "Umpire Sick With Remorse," an item out of Brazil, Ind., reported that Mr. Badden, stricken with a bellyache, had made the diagnosis himself: "I must be suffering because of all the bad decisions I've made in my life."

Now, Mr. Badden is no acquaintance of this bystander but the heart goes out to him in his hour of pain. If he thinks he's nauseated now, wait until he starts hearing from friends. "At last," ball players all over the nation must be saying, "an umpire who has managed to turn his own stomach!"

Chances are a lot of fans merely glanced at the headline, asked themselves what was so unusual about that, for the love of Augie Donatelli, and went on to read about Robin Roberts. This merely indicates loose thinking on their part.

To be sure, umpires are subject to many of the same ailments that attack humans, but usually these seizures occur on the playing field with specialists in attendance on both benches, ready to diagnose the case and recommend remedies. Mr. Badden fell ill while traveling, presumably alone, without medical advice.

It is to be hoped that he will have recovered completely before these lines get into print. If not, attending physicians might be advised to call into consultation the distinguished Bavarian specialist, Dr. Franz Frisch, B.Sc., Fordham; M.D., Heidelberg; Ph.D., Pilsen-with-an-egg-in-it.

Though he is not now in active practice, Dr. Frisch is recognized as the world's foremost authority on the afflictions of umpires, and his sprightly monograph, "Psycholepsy in Psychasthenic Individuals and Its Effect Upon the Neurospongium or Inner Reticular Stratum of the Retina," is regarded as the definitive work in this field.

When he was Chief Resident in Sportsman's Park, St. Louis, and subsequently in Wrigley Field, Chicago, and Forbes Field, Pittsburgh, Dr. Frisch was especially noted for his brilliantly rapid diagnosis, particularly in cases involving myopic astigmatism. On one occasion, musing in the dugout, he employed some abstruse medical terms in a ringing tone that reached the ears of the umpire behind the plate.

The umpire whipped off his mask and whirled to face

36

the great scientist. "What did you say?" he demanded truculently.

"Himmel!" said Dr. Frisch after a shocked pause. "Don't tell me you're deaf, too!"

Almost equally renowned in this field is the French scholar, Dr. L. Ernest duRocher, D.D., West Springfield Seminary, NBC-TV, famed especially for his work with anxiety neuroses and sophomania, or delusions of omniscience. He, too, has temporarily retired from active practice to the west coast, where he is engaged in research experiment with apes.

Umpires who consulted Dr. duRocher complained occasionally of his brusque bedside manner and insisted that the treatments he prescribed were worse than the ailments they suffered. Dr. duRocher's professional colleagues, however, say he has a heart of gold, mostly Horace Stoneham's.

In any event, Mr. Badden should be warned against any attempt to treat himself with home remedies. When the late Bill McGowan was an umpire in the American League, he cited the tragic case of an umpire named Mike with whom he had worked in the Eastern League.

Like Mr. Badden, Mike had a conscience; like him, Mike called some bad decisions in his time; these led, inevitably, to periodic fits of depression. After one particularly untidy rhubarb, he was inconsolable. This, he told Bill in the dressing room, was the end. The league president's patience had worn thin, anyhow, and there'd surely be a telegram of dismissal in the morning.

Deaf to Bill's words of comfort, Mike went out that night and applied medication. He continued to apply it right on through the darkness and into the dawn, and when he reported for work the next afternoon it required no specialist to diagnose his condition.

There were only two umpires assigned to a game in those days but Bill told Mike to go back to the hotel and let him work alone. No, Mike said, if Bill would just lead him to the foul line he could find his way out the stripe to his position at first base.

Bill complied and Mike assumed his stance near the bag, arms folded and chin outthrust. On the very first

37

batter there was a hairline play at first base. Mike didn't twitch.

"What is he, Mike? Out or safe?" There was no answer. First baseman, coach and runner converged on the umpire. He stood statuesque and immobile, his eyes fixed on a point somewhere beyond the horizon.

"Mike! Mike! What is he?"

"What is he!" Mike roared. "Hell's bells! *Where* is he?"

More Fresh Money? .. Sal Maglie

May 1956   New York

There is absolutely nothing to the report that the Dodgers got Sal Maglie to have him stuffed and mounted in the plastic dome atop O'Malley Gardens. The deal may puzzle baseball fans, but figuring it out is child's play for any psychologist. Some scars never heal, some fears never subside. Even today, the Dodgers got to have Maglie where they can keep an eye on him.

For some of us eldering gaffers, it's a joy to see the old boy rescued from the wilds of darkest Ohio. It is comforting to know that the big town takes care of its own, stands ever ready to provide a straw pallet and crackers and milk for an aging buck, with maybe even a seat on a park bench alongside Barney Baruch.

Speaking of us pensioners, some facts have been learned lately about the social security situation in baseball. It is frequently alleged that the public memory is short. Well, do fans remember what a bobbery was kicked up only a few years back about the ball players' pension plan? There was, if you do remember, the very hell of a fuss, with the players yelling for an immediate increase in benefits and the owners threatening to scuttle the pension arrangements entirely, and Ford Frick in the middle getting belted from both sides.

On the issue of increasing the benefits, the commissioner held firm. There must be no additional commitments, he said, until those already made could be paid for. At that time the pension system was about $4,500,-000 in arrears, or, more accurately, that much more cash was needed in the tin box before financial security would be achieved.

Very quietly since then, that security has been achieved. The four and a half million has now been made up, or will be this year. What was only a plan a few years ago is a reality now. Come war or deluge or stock market collapse, the ball player is assured that at the age of fifty he will start collecting whatever payments he has qualified for up to $100 a month.

In today's economy, of course, $100 a month represents something less than the wealth of the Indies. But if there is a more liberal arrangement in any industry it has not come to attention here. Benefits begin at the extraordinarily early age of fifty. And a man becomes eligible for the minimum of $50 a month after only five years of major league service. A ten-year man gets the maximum. This isn't counting such advantages as insurance which even a one-year man can have. Considering that baseball is a tiny business by comparison with scores of other concerns, the ball players and the owners have right to be proud of what they have accomplished. It makes their quarreling of a few years back seem even sillier than it seemed then.

With the budget now balanced and with sound reason to anticipate increased income in the future, the question of what to do with the fresh money is, of course, bound to come up.

For five years, television sponsors have been paying $1,000,000 for the World Series. On the next contract, they may pay two or three million.

Baseball has been putting $800,000 a year plus interest into the pension fund to get it on a firm footing. Hereafter it's going to cost something like $500,000 a year to keep the system operating, which means there'll be some loose change left over in this quarter.

Perhaps the players will decide that the time is now ripe to fatten the pension system along the lines they favored a few years ago. Maybe they'll want to establish an even earlier retirement age, or jack up the monthly payments, or both. It isn't possible to say here how far they might reasonably go in this direction; actuarial figures are essential to such a decision.

Ever since radio and television began to make substantial contributions to the World Series take, there has been a notion here that some of this new income could be used to right a wrong—or, let's say, to remedy a situation that has always seemed to be an unfortunate one.

When the money is available, why shouldn't there be a standard purse for the teams competing in the World Series? As all fans know, the players' pool comes out of the receipts of the first four World Series games. In 1954 those games were played in the spacious Polo Grounds and Cleveland's Municipal Stadium; the winning players got $11,147.90 each. In 1918 the Red Sox got $1,102.51 each for winning the world championship, though that would not happen today.

There is something intrinsically wrong when a member of the Red Sox, say, has to take a thousand or so less than a Yankee would get for winning a World Series, just on account of architecture. With television money to underwrite the risk, there seems no good reason why the players' pool couldn't be pegged at a comfortable figure that wouldn't vary.

Most fans are unaware that there is a minimum World Series purse guaranteed. It figures out to about $4,000 to each winning player and $2,500 to each loser, varying according to the number of shares voted by the players.

Trouble is, the guarantee isn't big enough.

Victoria is a State of Mind

May 1956   Hollywood

What every young man should know if he's going to Australia, said Miss Victoria Shaw, is that he ought to leave his bride at home. This the travel folders do not

40

tell people who are considering a junket to the Olympic Games next winter.

"Nevertheless," Miss Shaw said firmly, "it is true. American men have no trouble in Australia. The women all love them and the men all hate them. Really, it's serious. Australian girls are frightfully keen about Americans. It's the accent that gets them."

It wasn't only the accent that got the males who were listening to Miss Victoria Shaw, though when she spoke it was like a mountain brook singing through this dimly lit Hollywood bistro. What got them was Miss Victoria Shaw herself, lovelier than a Neopolitan sunset.

Miss Victoria Shaw is a doll baby from Australia who is going to make America's movie audiences wonder where Sydney has been all these centuries. A year ago she had a walk-on bit in a parade of mannequins that made part of a show Bob Hope was doing Down Under. Out of that came a chance to visit New York—to study television techniques, she thought, and go home and produce some shows—and as soon as she landed, the movie scouts began to vibrate.

"Wow!" they said. So here she is in Hollywood. Working for Columbia in "The Eddie Duchin Story." (She's Eddie's second wife, Chiquita, who also spoke in British accents.)

Now she was taking time away from the lot to tell some benighted Yankees what they might expect if they were to attend the Olympics.

"The weather," she said cheerily, "will be shocking. The temperature will be 105 one day and miserably raw the next. You won't like the hotels or the scenery."

The way she said it, it all sounded enchanting.

"Oh, yes," she said. "You should be warned that the bars in Melbourne close at 6 p.m. They call it—" her expression suggested distaste—"the 'six o'clock swill.' Down home, you see, we don't have cocktail lounges like yours here. Women aren't allowed in our bars.

"Most people finish work about 5 o'clock and they rush to the hotels and bars and, of course, they know they must drink fast because of the 6 o'clock closing. So

41

they get—" Miss Victoria Shaw shrugged a pretty Shavian shrug.

Well, now, as to sports—

"We're frightfully keen about tennis and racing," she said. "At the time of the Melbourne Cup, which is like your Kentucky Derby, there'll be no hotel accommodations at all. Football, too, only ours is Rugby League, much rougher than your football.

"A team of American college players came down for a game under Australian rules. The Australian players, you know, don't wear any protective covering at all, even though it's so rough. When the crowd saw the Yankees come out with all that thick padding here and here, and then when they started their preliminary exercises—well, my dear; you never heard anything like it.

"Baseball? No, we don't have any. The closest approach is a kind of cross between cricket and vigoro, which is played chiefly by women—"

"In this country," Miss Shaw was told, "Vigoro is a plant food."

"Really?" she said. "You do have some odd foods in America."

"A man told me," one of the worshippers said, "that I should go to New Zealand for the fishing."

"If you like fishing," she said, "you'll love New Zealand. It's so lovely, so green. It always looks, and the air always tastes, as though it just stopped raining a moment ago. Ah, it's glorious. You'll love New Zealand."

"Yes, but Australia and the kangaroos—"

"The kangaroo," Miss Shaw said, "is a dreadful pest. Breaks down fences and so on. In some sections there's a bounty on them, but it's almost impossible to shoot one. If you do get one, you're likely to find about twenty bullet holes in him."

"By the way," she said, "be sure to bring your own cigarettes and coffee. There's no such thing in Australia as a decent cup of coffee."

She smiled. When Miss Victoria Shaw smiles, Sanka tastes delicious.

What Has Football To Do With College?

May 1956   New York

The more the papers publish about labor conditions in college football on the Pacific Coast, the more clearly does the reader appreciate the evils of coddling hired hands. The fact is, they pay their help too much out there; the bums aren't worth what they've been getting.

Perhaps an exception should be made for the University of California at Los Angeles. If U.C.L.A. has been paying the top dollar, nobody can argue that the money has been ill spent. For several years, U.C.L.A. has had one of the very best football teams in the country.

It would be difficult to say as much for the other teams in the Pacific Coast Conference. How big was that roll that some booster outfit connected with Southern California is supposed to have slid under the table to cheer and comfort meaty Trojans? The figure quoted was something over $71,000.

Not very many years ago $71,000 would have taken care of the entire payroll of the Philadelphia Eagles with enough left over for Bert Bell, the owner, to throw a hell of a party at Benny the Bum's and even then, bad as they were, the Eagles could have creamed an All-Star team recruited from the overpaid, overprivileged Pacific Coast Conference.

To the onlooker, there was something abhorrent about the lip-smacking enthusiasm with which the conference brass lowered the boom on U.C.L.A. Maybe it was simply a case of sincere educators endeavoring to protect academic standards, but the job was done with the obscene gusto of professionals seizing on a chance to break up the Yankees. By fining U.C.L.A. $15,000 and putting its teams in quarantine for three years, the conference created an impression that the school had been a lone sinner in a congress of saints. On the coast you are told that U.C.L.A.'s real crime was winning, that its *modus operandi* differed in no important respect from that of the lodge brothers.

Like the Yankees, U.C.L.A. appears to have offended the other league members by getting better results out of similar methods. Additionally, the college nettled investigators by doing their work for them. When the conference's hired cop wanted to inquire into the care and feeding of athletes on the campus, U.C.L.A. authorities said, "Don't bother, we'll do it for you," and did, and forwarded the findings to headquarters.

After U.C.L.A. was fined, put on three-year probation and ordered to keep paws out of the Rose Bowl swag, all resident members of the football squad were declared ineligible unless they could prove that they hadn't been getting paid over the conference wage scale. Evidently that flighty notion about the presumption of innocence hasn't managed to scale the Rockies.

The old question of defining labor's fair share in the fruits of labor is a continuing problem in college football. There is something scandalous about a college collecting hundreds of thousands in gate receipts and paying off the help with a bowl of rice. Yet to give the players an equitable slice of the profits they make possible would destroy the conception of sport as an amusement for undergraduates.

It would also unbalance the budget. Many colleges would be better off without vast and expensive athletic plants, but many don't realize that until the stadia and field houses are built. Then, saddled with debt, they've got to operate football as big business or go bankrupt.

There was widespread shock a quarter of a century ago when the Carnegie report disclosed that some colleges were paying their athletes. Memory recreates that time as an age of innocence when undergraduates were proud of their teams and resented any implication that their school would compromise amateur standards. At many schools today, the students resent the athletes.

During the last Christmas holidays there was a flock of kids around from a college whose teams have ranked in recent years among the best that money could buy.

These kids regarded the athletes with mild, amused contempt.

They didn't object to the players' presence on the campus and it was no concern of theirs that the players received financial aid and weren't required to meet academic standards. They rather enjoyed having a good team to entertain them on Saturdays.

As for old-fashioned sentiments, like loyalty and pride in the old school, that was out of their line. Football? What did that have to do with college?

The Bleeding Hearts and Dave Sime

June 1956   New York

If Dave Sime is unable to qualify for the Olympics—and the chances are the combined talents of Ben Jones, Mr. Fitz and Max Hirsch couldn't get him ready—then just as sure as amateur sport makes little applehead, there is going to be an outcry against the American method of selecting a team. The bleeding-hearts will make no sense but their noise will be deafening.

Sime is the red-headed outfielder who went to Duke to play baseball and remained to shatter the watches of timers clocking sprint races. One week after he had run 220 yards in world record time of 20 seconds, he pulled up sore in the National Collegiate Athletic Association championship in Berkeley, Calif., last Saturday.

He pulled a groin muscle running second to Bobby Morrow at 100 meters, and though this position qualified him for the final Olympic trials in that event, he was not able to compete at 200. Barring extraordinarily swift recovery, he will miss the Amateur Athletic Union championship in Bakersfield this week end, which is his only remaining opportunity to qualify in the 200, and there is grave doubt that he will be fit a week later for the Olympic finals at 100.

If that happens, then under the rules he may not go to Melbourne in November except as a tourist paying his own fare. It will be a grievous disappointment to him but an irresistible opportunity for the professional scolds of press and radio to horse-whip our Olympic officials.

"This couldn't happen in Russia," the bleeding-hearts will cry. "Are those stuffed shirts trying to throw the games to the Reds?"

This expresses a curious form of reasoning employed not only in sports but in many other quarters, including our courts and legislative halls. The very persons who make the eagle scream loudest, who shout with every breath their abhorrence of all things Russian, are frequently the first to hold up the Russian method as a model for us to follow.

Russia, these logicians point out, never would let a silly rule disqualify the nation's greatest sprinter from its Olympic team. Why, then, should we be so foolish? Those who argue thus seldom know their facts, probably would not be aware that Sime—brilliant though his promise is—has not yet established himself as America's greatest sprinter and might very well be beaten off if he were fit to run in the final tryouts.

Neither does it occur to them that the fact that our rules would be rejected in Russia may be a compelling argument in favor of honoring them here. If we approve the American way, why are we always hankering after the Communist way?

The American system of trial-by-competition is a reflection of the wealth of talent in this country. Nations with sparser material arbitrarily choose for the Olympics the athletes who, on the basis of past performance, are deemed likeliest to win. Our men must survive a series of eliminations and arrive at an officially designated place on a designated day prepared to finish one-two-three in the final trial.

In a nation that has four or more men capable of winning the 100 in the Olympics, this is the only fair method. Otherwise, an indefensible injustice would be done to one of the four.

If Sime loses his chance because of injury, fans will grieve for him. But suppose the rules were waived and, after the finals, the kid who finished third were told: "Nice try, sonny, but we're putting you back in your

46

box. You know as well as we do that Sime can run faster than you."

The kid could properly reply: "He can, huh? Let him get out here on the track and prove it."

Matter of fact, if our men qualified on reputation rather than performance, the ruling Olympic sprint champion might be Herb McKenley of Jamaica. A committee of handicappers might easily have chosen somebody like Andy Stanfield or Jim Gathers over Lindy Remigino, in 1952, but Remigino won his ride to Helsinki by finishing second to Art Bragg in the trials. In Finland Bragg went lame and Remigino beat McKenley in a photo.

When they weep over Sime and plead for an exception in his favor, nobody will be shedding tears over Jim Golliday, who is in the same boat. Northwestern's sprinter, probably our top man on proven ability, broke down in March.

Physical injury is a hazard in every sport. To win, you've got to be there and compete. There isn't any other way.

Ted Williams Spits; Gussie Moran Comments

August 1956   New York

By now some modern Dickens, probably in Boston, must surely have brought out a best seller entitled, "Great

47

Expectorations." It was a $4,998 mistake when Ted Williams chose puritanical and antiseptic New England for his celebrated exhibition of spitting for height and distance. In easy-going New York's insanitary subway the price is only $2.

It was bush, of course. There is no other way to characterize Williams' moist expression of contempt for fans and press, even though one may strive earnestly to understand and be patient with this painfully introverted, oddly immature thirty-eight-year-old veteran of two wars.

In his gay moods, Williams has the most winning disposition and manner imaginable. He can be charming, accommodating and generous. If Johnny Orlando, the Red Sox maitre de clubhouse and Ted's great friend, wished to violate a confidence he could cite a hundred instances of charities that the fellow has done, always in deep secrecy.

This impulsive generosity is a key. Ted is ruled by impulse and emotions. When he is pleased he laughs; in a tantrum, he spits. In Joe Cronin's book, this falls $5,000 short of conduct becoming a gentleman, officer and left-fielder.

The price the Boston general manager set upon a minute quantity of genuine Williams saliva, making it the most expensive spittle in Massachusetts, suggests that the stuff is rarer than rubies. However, this is one case where the law of supply and demand does not apply.

Actually the $5,000 figure is a measure of Cronin's disapproval of his employee's behavior and an indication of Ted's economic condition. Rather than let the punishment fit the crime, Cronin tailored it to the outfielder's $100,000 salary. As it is, considering Williams' tax bracket, chances are the Federal government will pay about $3,500 of the fine, though it may cause some commotion around the Internal Revenue Bureau when a return comes in with a $5,000 deduction for spit.

Baseball has indeed put on company manners since the days when pitchers like Burleigh Grimes, Clarence Mitchell and Spittin' Bill Doak employed saliva as a tool of the trade and applied it to the ball with the ceremonious formality of a minuet.

48

Incidentally, the penalty was applied after Williams drew a base on balls which forced home the winning run for Boston against the Yankees. He must have realized that a few more victories at those prices would leave him broke, yet the next night he won another game with a home run. With Ted, money is no object.

Nobody has ever been able to lay down a rule determining how much abuse a paid performer must take from the public without reciprocation. It was either Duffy or Sweeney, of the great old vaudeville team, who addressed an audience that had sat in cold silence through the act:

"Ladies and gentlemen, I want to thank you for giving us such a warm and encouraging reception. And now, if you will kindly remain seated, my partner will pass among you with a baseball bat and beat the bejabbers out of you."

Baseball fans consider that the price they pay for admission entitles them to spit invective at a player, harass him at his work and even bounce a beer bottle off his skull. It is not recalled that Williams' hair was ever parted by flying glassware, but verbal barbs from Fenway Park's left-field seats have been perforating his sensitive psyche for years.

There are those of a sympathetic turn who feel it was high time Williams be permitted to spit back. Miss Gussie Moran, trained in the gentle game of tennis, remarked on the radio that she approved, "as long as he didn't spray anybody." As in tennis, Gussie believes, marksmanship and trajectory count.

All the same it is a mark of class in a performer to accept cheers and jeers in stride. One of the solider citizens of the Boston press—it could have been Johnny Drohan—pointed this out to Williams years ago. Ted was a kid then, a buff for Western movies.

Hoots and jeers were a part of the game, the man said, and everybody in the public eye had to learn to accept them.

"Take actors, for instance, Ted. You see one in a good show and you applaud and go around talking about how great he is. Then you see him in a bad vehicle and you say, 'He stinks. Whatever gave me the idea he could act?' "

"Oh, no, Johnny," Ted protested, "not that Hoot Gibson. He's *always* great!"

Swaps, Princess Kelly and a Mrs. Smith

September 1956   Atlantic City

A delectable blonde named Mrs. Grimaldi, and a chestnut horse named Swaps, royal refugees from the court of Sam Goldwyn, underwent narrowly critical scrutiny from something like 28,000 pairs of eyes this gray and gusty afternoon. While the tote board of the Atlantic City race course glowed like a winner at Monte Carlo, Swaps was scheduled in the $100,000 United Nations Handicap with Princess Grace of Monaco looking on with her spouse.

The customers gazed on Her Serene Highness and hoped to gamble on His Sunkissed Magnificence, which was in both cases exactly what wise nature had in mind when she designed them. However, Swaps was a last-minute scratch.

The United Nations, a mile and three-sixteenths on grass for a winner's purse of $65,000, was the first Eastern appearance, Florida excepted, for the record-smashing champion of Hollywood Park. Under 130 pounds, he was giving up fifteen pounds to some first-rate competitors, and in ordinary circumstances this would have made him the cynosure of all eyes not preoccupied with the past performance charts.

This time, however, he got only a share of the spotlight due to the presence of Jack Kelly's little girl Grace, former queen of the Sunset Strip and now a Princess on the Cote D'Azur. The Princess was fetching in a gray suit and bright red cossack turban. The horse wore Willie Shoemaker in red and black silks.

Horse players found this clearing in the Jersey pines aflutter with the flags of thirteen nations and at the finish line the seats reserved for Frank D. Fiore, a director of the track, had been transformed by bunting into a royal box. On display there were the colors of the United States and the *rouge et blanc* of Monaco, whose flag doesn't pay off on *noir*.

Breathless couriers reported, shortly after 12:30 p.m., that all was serene and high downstairs, where the track president's daughter and her groom were lunching with the nobility of Philadelphia.

"She's lovely," a spy said, "but the Prince looks kinda glum."

"Probably worrying about whether it'll be a boy," a clocker suggested.

On the clubhouse lawn, gawkers stood with their backs to the running strip, staring at the still unoccupied royal box. The band played "Everywhere You Go," a favorite of Mr. Fiore, who entertains on the bull fiddle at parties, but eschewed his companion favorite, "Toot-Toot-Tootsie, Goodbye," this being a form of royal address not sanctioned by De Brett.

On a Minsky-type runway behind the box, models paraded in a fashion show while a female chart-caller on the public address system recited the form and breeding of the exhibits: "A red wool daytime dress with bloused back and brass buttons, by Molly Parnis."

A little before first post, business practically ceased at the mutuel windows. Everybody was down front craning for a serene and lofty view. The box remained untenanted. The band played "Love Is a Many Splendored Thing." Still no bride. "My Heart Stood Still," the musicians prompted, without response.

A trumpeter sounded "Boots and Saddles" for the first race, bringing a burst of excited applause. Instead of a Princess, there appeared from under the stands one Oliver Cutshaw on horseback, leading the parade to the post. At long last, three New Jersey troopers in their Graustarkian uniforms cut a path open and here came Grace and Rainier. Now the racing could start.

"I hope," snarled a horse player to his gaping bride, "you've got your $3.60 worth now." He turned and watched Longleat win the first heat at $12.

Mrs. Grimaldi, spies reported, had five $10 tickets on

the daily double. One coupled Longleat with Son O'Doge and would have been worth $2,118 if the latter had won the second race. Son O'Doge was out of the money behind Salmative. A Mrs. Smith, without a horse track or roulette wheel to her name, collected $27.20 on that double. As the poet says, all women are equal on the turf and under it.

KF-79 and Lou Little

September 1956   New York

When Branch Rickey, then landlord at Ebbets Field, impounded the trunks and torsos of the Brooklyn Football Dodgers, he invited Lou Little to write his own figures on a contract as coach. Lou was sorely tempted, thinking of all the Cashmere sweaters and Shetland sports jackets and doeskin slacks that a top wage in professional football could add to an already exquisite wardrobe, but at length he declined. Otherwise he would have been out of work seven years ago, for the Dodgers died untidily in 1949.

Due to Columbia University's mandatory retirement policy, he is going to be at liberty anyhow after the 1956 season. The age limit of sixty-five applies to everybody except halfbacks, not only to professors of romance languages but also to the man whose colleagues have called him "Columbia's best teacher." After twenty-seven years,

Coach Little has discovered the job was only temporary.

When they say "Columbia's best teacher" educators are not referring to Lou's gift for inducting the young into the mysteries of the belly series. They are thinking, rather, of the goals Lou always had in mind when he said, "I want men who will knock the other fellow's brains out, then help him up and brush him off."

They are thinking of what a kid had in mind as he pulled off his padded playsuit after the final game of his senior year. He would never play college football again. Showered and dressed for the street, he walked over to offer his hand to the coach. "Thank you, Mr. Little," he said, "for teaching me so much more than football."

Sports pages and alumni, as a rule, rank football coaches according to the number of games their teams win, a meaningless criterion. A far more accurate measure would be provided if one could count the hundreds of young men from Columbia and other colleges, amateurs and professionals and boys who never played any game, former proteges of Lou Little and strangers to him, who have written or called on him over the years seeking his help in the business of living.

Not even Lou can measure the influence he has exerted through his "Squad Letters," which he writes every six weeks and has mimeographed and mailed to the hundreds who played football for Columbia since he took charge in 1930.

To be a taskmaster who can lead and a martinet who inspires loyalty rather than resentment, that is a rare art. "Listen, you guys," Lou has told his players, "I don't want you ever to call anybody a guy. Sam 'man' or 'fellow.'"

If a kid came unshaven to Columbia's training table, no food passed his lips until a razor had cleared his chin. To the sartorially impeccable coach, the offense was heinous and the penalty extreme, for Lou has always run one-two-three with the greatest trenchermen on the Atlantic seaboard. Regretfully, he confesses today that he has slowed down; ordered pie a la mode for dessert where he used to take lamb chops.

Though Lou always declines to name any former player as his favorite lest he offend another, two who must have made him happy were Lou Kusserow and Gene Rossides. Probably they were the best two backs he ever had together. They were the last to quit the locker room after helping to defeat Syracuse in their final game in 1948, and they approached the coach together.

"Thank you," one of them said, "for everything you've done for us."

"I never did anything for you boys," Lou said, "you did everything for me."

They walked out together and Lou watched them go and he had to be remembering. He must have recalled the day when Army, unbeaten in thirty-two games, lost to the Columbia team of Kusserow and Rossides and, of course, Bill Swiacki. It was Swiacki, Bill Heinz said later, who caught passes "the way the rest of us catch common colds; he knows where he gets some, the rest he just picks up in a crowd."

Naturally, Lou remembers KF-79, but not quite the way most others remember it. This was, of course, the naked reverse on which "Pomona High," as Columbia was contemptuously called, whipped Stanford, 7 to 0, in the muddy Rose Bowl on Jan. 1, 1934.

What Lou and few others remember is that Columbia had tried the same play in the first quarter but Stanford's swift safety man had angled across the field and made a shoe-top tackle on the twelve-yard line.

When the play was called again on the seventeen-yard line, Owen McDowell, Columbia's left end, said to Larry Pinckney, the short-side guard: "This time you cross over and take my man, the right half. I'll go get the safety man."

If Stanford was horrified to see Al Barabas dash over for the winning touchdown, Lou was equally startled to find McDowell downfield smashing the safety man. Startled and delighted, he remembers it now with a secret pleasure as great as the pleasure of victory. He always tried to teach his guys to think for themselves. His fellows, that is.

What's Out of Bounds? The Clock?

October 1956   New York

With just a moment less than three minutes to play, Columbia's football team took a 6-point lead over Harvard and kicked off. The Harvards had a long way to go for a score and needed all the time they could get. Matt Botsford, the quarterback, threw a pass to Walt Stahura, his left half, who was tackled near the side line not far from the Columbia bench.

As soon as his forward progress was halted, Stahura flung the ball out of bounds with a little two-handed basket toss. Maybe somebody on the Columbia bench kicked the ball, although in the press box it was not possible to be sure of this. Anyhow, the ball bounded back onto the playing field and Stahura slapped it out again.

He was resolved to stop that clock and no nonsense about it.

Nobody raised a murmur. If there had been any comment, it would have been praise for Stahura for keeping his wits about him. Under the rules, time goes out when the ball goes out of bounds. Stahura saved Harvard the precious seconds which otherwise would have been consumed establishing a new line of scrimmage and getting the next play started.

If he had stopped the clock by faking injury instead of faking a fumble, the wowsers would have lifted a cry of "unethical practice."

If there is any difference at all between faking an injury and faking a fumble, the distinction is too fine for these myopic eyes. The purpose of both is precisely the same—to gain time for one or more additional plays which might win the ball game. (As it turned out, the Harvards didn't score and Stahura's quick thinking didn't help them, but he was in there trying.)

There is no rule against fumbling or faking a fumble.

There is no rule against breaking a leg or faking an injury. The latter, however, is officially designated as malpractice and the coach whose operatives employ the strategem is deemed a low fellow unfit to wolf lasagna with his more spiritual brethren in Gene Leone's pizzeria.

Theoretically, deliberate fumbling involves the risk of losing possession but in practice the risk is less than negligible. Any player in possession of the ball and his faculties can flip the thing safely out of bounds a thousand times in a thousand tries when the sideline is only a few feet away. Some coaches make their men practice it, and nobody accuses them of teaching sharp practice.

When a player simulates injury, the wowsers cry "sham! fraud! deceit!" and that's what it is, of course. Yet is it deeper dishonesty to say "ouch!" when you don't hurt than to say "oops! it slipped," when it didn't? Truth, they used to teach us, is absolute.

When Harvard's last sally failed and Columbia took possession, Claude Beham ate up the remaining time running plays into the line with no thought of gaining ground but only to hold the ball until the game should end. Had he done otherwise, had he flung the ball around at the risk of an interception and possible touchdown run, he would have been unworthy of the noble calling of quarterback.

Yet honestly, what's the difference between deliberately stopping the clock to save time and purposely keeping it running to use time up? Frequently in the closing minutes you'll see the team in front dawdling overlong in the huddle, straggling sluggishly out of it, taking penalties for delay of the game if necessary, just so time runs out.

In at least one classic case, a team argued away the other side's last chance. It was a Penn-Michigan game which Michigan had in hand until the late stages when Penn's passes started clicking. The Penns got a touchdown that cut their deficit to two or three points with less than a minute remaining, and of course had to kick off. They tried the only tactic possible, a short kick-off, and they recovered it legally.

Immediately, Michigan formed an argumentative ring around the referee, the late, great Bill Crowell, and Penn kids were still frantically trying to break through and call time out when the game ended. Bill Crowell defended himself on the ground that no time-out was sought but he was a dead level guy. Privately he admitted that he had booted one by not taking time out himself to save Penn the chance Penn had earned.

The point it seems here, is that a football game should not be measured by time. It isn't a game of continuous action like ice hockey. The rules provide for sixty minutes of play, but actually the ball is in play far less than sixty minutes.

There are plenty of statistics available on the average number of plays which two crisply moving teams can get into a fifteen-minute quarter. Rewrite the rules to allow that many plays to the period. Throw out the time clock and substitute a dial with a big hand that ticks off each play as it is made.

Then the team that controls the ball will wind up with the greater number of offensive plays, and when the last is made the game will be over. There'll be no stalling, no unseemly haste, and no scandalized cries from the wowsers.

Lost in Australia: XVI Olympiad

November 1956   Melbourne

Fair dinkum, which means cross my heart and hope to die, you'd have sworn half the population of Melbourne had set out before breakfast to ogle the athletes at Olympic Village in suburban Heidelberg. Motors clogged the streets and pedestrians by the thousands milled outside the gates of the wire-fenced compound thrusting autograph books into the paws of anybody who showed up wearing a sweatsuit. One athlete was caught in the throng like an Arctic whaler in an ice field. He'd scribble his name a dozen times, take one tentative stride forward and the crowd would close in and force him two strides back-ward.

"Would it be like this every day?" somebody asked Harold Blakey who was driving a party of visitors.

"Beg yours," he said. "Oh no, tomorrow they'll be back on their jobs, but today they've all got to come out and have a bit of stickynose. Chockablock, isn't it?"

Chockablock it was indeed, though inside the reservation the scene was tranquil enough. Olympic Village is a spacious housing development so new that grass is just beginning to sprout on freshly seeded lawns. Boys and girls from many nations strolled the streets. The unseemly bawl of an Elvis Presley recording shook the walls of the big recreation center but didn't seem to bother the kids playing checkers or cards there or reading or writing letters.

Andy Stanfield, the American sprinter, was playing chess with Boris Stolyarov, Russia's top man in the high hurdles. Stanfield got the Russian's king in check and looked up from the board.

"He's a nice guy," he said. "Should've seen him dancing with all the girls last night."

The English words meant nothing to Stolyarov but he knew from the tone that they were friendly and about him, and he grinned all over. Half a dozen moves later Stanfield had him checkmated, the first American victory over Russia in the Sixteenth Olympiad.

"Chess is their game too," Andy said. "Of course I played it all through college."

The way these young men are getting on, it made a fellow wonder at all this tension over the international situation which you read about. Does it have to affect the Olympic Games? Is this tripe necessary?

This is written after a conscientious and coldly scientific survey of Melbourne's most celebrated institution—the 6 o'clock swill. The Olympic Games will spawn bigger headlines in the world press, but the press of this troubled world is not noted for its sense of proportion. Take a bottle-scarred researcher's word for it, the Olympic marathon will produce no gamer competitors or pluckier stayers than the legions who rush the growler six evenings a week in Melbourne's pubs. The 6 o'clock swill is a charming folk custom sired by a law which requires saloons to stop serving at 6 p.m. This creates a challenge which no Aussie worth his malt will take lying down, or at least not as long as he can stand. Most offices close at five, most shops at five-thirty. It isn't easy to make your load in one hour, much less thirty minutes, but these people come from pioneer stock.

In a recent referendum a proposal to keep bars open until 10 o'clock was defeated by an odd coalition, not to say an unholy one. Marshaled against the bill were the outright prohibitionists, the saloonkeepers, and the housewives. The first group wants the joints closed as early as possible, the proprietors are happy with the roaring business they do and don't want working hours extended and labor costs increased. The wives just want their husbands.

"When my Joe comes home," the suburban ladies concede, "he's generally tiddly and sometimes rotten. But he does get home for supper."

Briefed on these simple, sordid facts, an exploring party set out at 5 p.m. guided by a Melbourne taxpayer whose feeling for the 6 o'clock swill is one of warm appreciation. "There's bound to be jostling," he said, "and you're odds on to slop some beer on another bloke. You say 'sorry.' When you've spilled enough beer on him you're friends for life. Makes it a quite decent social do, if you know what I mean."

First stop was the pub in Hosie's Hotel, an old place lately rebuilt, rather shiny with blond paneling. It's a fairly sizable room with two bars forming an L down the lefthand wall and across the back. Drinkers weren't three deep as they are in a good New York saloon in rush hours. They simply packed the joint from wall to wall, laborers, clerks, business men, truckers, here and there a sailor or soldier. All were males. "The women," the guide said, "are breaking down the barriers. It's only in the last five or six months that they've been showing up in pubs. By the time the games are over, I think it will be broken down altogether, except in a blood house like this. Toss that off and we'll go along."

He led the way down the street to the Port Philip Club Hotel, a long arcade with bars in the arcade proper and bars in rooms branching off to right and left. The place was jammed with sailors. When you ordered a beer, the barman didn't carry your glass to a tap. He carried a pistol-shaped spigot hitched to a long tube and squirted your glass full where you stood.

"For mass production," the guide said, "Detroit couldn't beat this. Would you call it Willow Run? Let's go meet Chloe."

Chloe is a gilt-framed blob of pink loveliness in Young and Jackson's pub a few doors down the street. She hangs on a battered, scaly wall, gloriously nude and internationally famous. She was painted in 1875 from a model—legend says—named Marie, a lively lady of Paris. The tale is told that one night Marie gathered all her friends for a lavish feast, wined them and dined them and sent them away, then boiled match heads into a poisonous potion and gulped it down.

It was getting on toward 6 o'clock and the jam in Young and Jackson's several bars was beyond describing. More than a few customers had heavy looking satchels, full of bottled beer that they would take home, the guide said. Six o'clock struck and a voice of dire warning came howling out of loudspeakers. Some drinkers lined up three or four glasses, for they would have fifteen minutes to empty them and clear out. A minute after six, men were pleading for one more and bartenders were opening the taps from which beer no longer flowed.

Downstairs somebody had shut off a master valve.

Here was the picture. At ten o'clock last night, women with sleeping infants in their arms sat among the crowds in temporary bleachers in front of Town Hall in Swanston Street. The board seats were hard but the rewards would be great. In a matter of fifteen hours, Philip Mountbatten, the Duke of Edinburgh, would be right there in the living, breathing flesh at the same hour citizens with box lunches and thermos bottles and sleeping bags were disposing themselves outside the gates of the Melbourne Cricket Ground. They'd have only twelve hours to wait before the doors would open and admit them to standing room inside. Then another five hours on their feet in aisles or clinging to stairways, and they'd be able to see and hear the Duke pronounce the sixteen words which he was traveling 16,000 miles to speak:

"I declare open the Olympic Games of Melbourne celebrating the XVI Olympiad of the modern era."

Mind you, where they stood there wasn't a brass rail to rest a foot on, and nobody was making them do it.

The Melbourne Cricket Ground, 103 years old, is an oddly impressive hybrid of antiquity and the atomic age. Seen from the outside, the double-decked old stands of weathered red brick suggest nothing so much as a brewery in South St. Louis. Grafted onto them is a sleek new addition of battleship gray, triple-decked and as modern as penicillin. Inside—at some of the busier gates it required almost an hour to get inside because the entrances were designed strictly for Eddie Arcaro—inside the towering cliffs were piebald with people as early as 11 a.m. There wasn't a great deal for them to see except a bright green meadow inclosed by a bright red track, and a scoreboard bearing the rather starry-eyed notion of Baron Pierre de Coubertin that: "The Olympic movement tends to bring together in a radiant union all the qualities which guide mankind to perfection." Beneath this effluvium from the founder of the modern Olympics was a reminder to the jingoists who try to picture this muscle dance as a head-on collision of democratic and Communist idealogies: "Classification of points on a national basis is not recognized." In other words, this is for fun, and no death struggle between the United States and Russia.

Well, sir, great gaggles of bands paraded and postured, playing "Waltzing Matilda" until a fellow's feet hurt, and exactly at 3 p.m. the Duke arrived. He sat alone in the back seat of an open car which made a horseshoe loop of the track, an unmeasured 300 yards, in 1:56.1, not good time for a Humber.

When the car stopped, a Boy Scout stepped up to open the door, so stiffly formal that the crowd laughed happily, and the Duke got out and just ambled across the

61

turf, casual as anything. He was wearing his sailor suit, all aglitter with gold braid. He stood at attention while a band played "God Save the Queen," shook hands with Olympic brass and disappeared under the stands, to show up twenty-five minutes later in the royal box.

Now the teams marched in, the muscular delegates of sixty-seven nations. Greece was first as always, on account of having perpetrated the Olympics first. The host nation is always last. In between, there are some odd ones, including us. Maybe the oddest thing of all is the attraction this pageant has. Once competition starts there are always empty seats. It's this fancy dress folderol that drags 'em in.

The leader of the Greek delegation was George Roubanis, a pole vaulter who is a sophomore at U.C.L.A. The Bulgarians had tan uniforms, some darker than others, as though some had been to the cleaners.

The Duke stood at attention, returning salutes even when salutes weren't given. Czechoslovakia, for one, neglected to dip her flag passing royalty but dipped it farther on down for Hungary. Prominent in the United States crowd was a blond kid chewing gum fiercely. Russia came in on the Yankees' heels; out of respect for Nina Ponomareva, the lady who lifted those berets in London, the Russian dolls were bareheaded.

As rigidly formalized as a minuet, the pageant rolled out. The brass talked. Bands played and pigeons were sprung from a battery of cages and a kid named Ron Clarke, the best young miler in the world, dashed around the track carrying the Olympic torch. Leaving the track he burrowed through the stands and reappeared on a kind of breezeway connecting two sections of seats, where he tossed his torch into a gilded gaboon that looked a little like a trash incinerator. Thanks to the Gas and Fuel Corporation of Victoria, the flame leapt from this dingy urn, and will leap until the gas man turns it off . . .

The cab driver was swart and solid and he looked tough, like a guy who might have grown up mixing it in the streets with Bobo Olson in the days before romance tenderized Bobo like one of those assembly-line hams. On the drive from the airport to the Royal Hawaiian Hotel he asked casually, "What was wrong with our team down there?" He meant down in Melbourne, of course, for the plane he had met was obviously carrying passengers from the Olympics.

"Nothing was wrong," his fare said. "Except in boxing, the Americans did as well as ever in the sports they care about, and in some cases better than ever.

"You've been reading about the Russians, of course. Well, they had a fine team and they did well. Where they piled up most of their points was in gymnastics and women's athletics and fields like that where we have no strength and don't particularly want any."

"Oh," the driver said, "that's how it was, eh?"

In the hotel there was a newspaper with the wrap-up story on the games as furnished by a wire service. It carried an eight-column banner reading: "Russia Wins Olympics." The dispatch reported that by the news service's unofficial point system, by the total of gold, silver and bronze medals accumulated by any other measure you chose to use. Russia had wound up the quadrennial love feast with a higher score than any other nation.

So there it was again.

Undoubtedly the same story was published in hundreds of other newspapers. It was an accurate recital of the facts, as far as it went. It omitted only one salient fact —that Olympic teams are not organized as national groups and the competition is not intended to pit nation against nation—else why should Luxembourg or Pakistan or Fiji bother entering a few athletes against the might of Russia, the United States or Australia?

For the hundredth but, regrettably, probably not the last time, let it be said that no country ever wins the

Olympics, notwithstanding whatever you may read to the contrary. Then having made that point let's admit that nobody's ever going to pay any attention to it.

Because nobody ever does pay any attention to it. "The Honolulu Advertiser" has stated editorially that "there is serious question as to the desirability of continuing the Olympic Games." The insistence on employing a non-existent scoring system puts some nations on top, others in subordinate positions, and this—says the editorial—"creates a rivalry that is injurious to the purpose sought."

Probably that's true, though the remedy suggested— abandoning the Olympics—is a good deal like shooting a dog to rid him of fleas. This is, after all, fun and games for children, and it isn't the play that makes trouble. It's the people who confuse sport with war.

What makes all the breast-beating doubly foolish is the fact that the Olympics include such a wide variety of individual and team competitions that it is flatly impossible to devise any equitable over-all scoring system. It will remain impossible until some mathematician manages to multiply apples by steam yachts and express the answer in yards.

As the games were closing, Jesse Abramson brought up one aspect of this situation in a press conference with Avery Brundage, president of the International Olympic Committee. He pointed out that in winning the decathlon championship, Milton Campbell excelled all others in eight of the ten events. He received one gold medal, not eight.

In gymnastics, however, it is possible for one contestant to win eight gold medals in eight separate events, plus one for over-all excellence, plus a tenth for membership in the winning team. Brundage agreed that this seemed less than an ideal arrangement and said maybe the I.O.C. could get around to doing something about it one of these eons.

Weaknesses of the "unofficial" scoring systems may be even more graphically illustrated thus: By winning the numbing ten-event competition which is the decathlon,

Campbell scored ten points for the United States; in gymnastics alone, Russians scored 180-odd points.

This, then, is how a nation "wins the Olympics," and if anybody can gain satisfaction from such a "victory," if anybody is disposed to get all chop-fallen about such a "defeat," then that ought to be his privilege.

As to the argument that Communists capitalize on such successes for propaganda purposes, this has not seemed a valid reason for panic here. It is cudgeling the obvious into a quivering jelly to say that excellence in the ladies' javelin throw does not prove the Soviet way of life better or worse than the democratic.

Jackie Robinson

December 1956   New York

Jackie Robinson could have quit baseball last year or this year or next and it would have occasioned no astonishment. To those who have known him and were aware of what pride he took in his skill, it seemed altogether reasonable that when he saw those gifts fading he would walk out. Somehow, the idea of him being traded always seemed outlandish.

It is impossible to think of Robinson except as a Dodger. Other players move from team to team and can change uniform as casually as the Madison Avenue space cadet shucks his weekday flannels for his week-end Bermuda shorts.

Robinson, though, has been a special case. His arrival in Brooklyn was a turning point in the history and the character of the game; it may not be stretching things to say it was a turning point in the history of this country.

It might have happened in any other town, but the fact is it happened in Brooklyn, and it will never be possible to disassociate Robinson and the Dodgers. They put their ineradicable brand on him, and nobody can ever deny that he has left his mark on the Dodgers.

He played for Brooklyn for ten seasons. In every single one of those years, the Dodgers either won the championship or led the race into September. It wasn't Jackie alone who kept 'em up there of course, but the blindest bigot in Georgia wouldn't dispute the statement that he has played a major role in the team's success.

The possibility that he might be traded never seemed remote to Robinson himself. Away back when Burt Shotton was managing Brooklyn, Jackie dropped a remark to the effect that Brooklyn probably would make some personnel changes for the following season and he wouldn't be surprised if he were sent elsewhere.

Next day in the Dodgers' dugout all the newspaper men were quizzing Shotton about the story and he was saying it was a lot of nonsense which he wouldn't dignify with comment. Then Jackie came along, was asked whether he'd been misquoted and in front of the manager he said positively not; he had said exactly what he'd been quoted as saying and he still thought it was true and wasn't going to take back a word.

But it was to the rest of us—the fans and newspaper men and guys in baseball—that the idea of Brooklyn letting Robinson go seemed fantastic. Most of us thought he would play for the Dodgers as long as he was able to play well, and that when that time passed his pride would tell him to walk away.

"Pride," he was saying one day. "No, I don't think pride has much to do with the way a man plays."

"But you're a proud player, Jackie," Roger Kahn said.

"I," Jackie said simply, "I am a proud fella."

So now Robinson is a Giant, and presumably a proud one. Not even Jackie can foretell whether he'll be worth what the Giants gave for him—a relief pitcher named Dick Littlefield and cash variously estimated at $30,000 to $50,000.

The only thing certain sure is that he can't hurt the Giants. He may not have much left, but what he has must be good. Does that also mean that the Dodgers without Robinson must be weaker than they were when they had him? Chances are it does, even if the Brooklyn Brainbund reasons otherwise. One cannot put down a suspicion that Robinson's departure represents the end of an era in Brooklyn. He is the first of the old guard to go, the first important defection from the company that has tyrannized the National League for a decade.

There can't be much time left for Pee Wee Reese and Roy Campanella and Carl Furillo and Duke Snider, and no matter how optimistic the Brooklyn club may be about young men coming up through the organization, none can qualify as a Robinson or Reese or Campanella or Snider or Furillo until he has shown his credentials in major league competition.

January 1957   New York

If it is true as it appears to be that Jackie Robinson has, for a price, deliberately crossed his friends and employers past and present, then it requires an eloquent advocate, indeed to make a convincing defense for him. From here, no defense at all is discernible.

By selling the news of his retirement from baseball to "Look" magazine and holding the announcement for that publication's deadline, he has embarrassed the Dodgers, dislocated the plans of the Giants and deceived the working newspaper men whose friendship he had and who thought they had his confidence.

Of all the various qualities which Robinson has displayed in the past, the most attractive was candor. In the end it was candor that he sacrificed to mislead the club that brought him into baseball and paid him for eleven years, the club that committed itself in good faith to pay him this year, and the individual members of a press that has contributed hugely to his fame.

As to his newspaper friends, "I think they will understand," he has said, "why this was one time I couldn't give them the whole story as soon as I knew it." He is probably correct. Those who feel he has flimflammed them will understand that he did it for money.

Because of his fiercely combative temperament rather than because of his color, Robinson has been frequently in the midst of controversy. A certain amount of adverse criticism necessarily resulted, but in the main he has had an extraordinarily favorable press, more favorable, perhaps, than that of any other equally stormy sports figure.

The newspaper men did not, of course, make him a great ball player. Nothing did that for him save his own skills and intelligence and resolution, though the press did spread and celebrate his fame. Giving him only the credit he earned but giving that ungrudgingly, the press helped make him a figure of distinction and when he was involved in controversy he was never without public defenders.

It's a matter of individual opinion whether this put him under any obligation to men who were merely doing their job. Walter O'Malley appears to feel that it did, for his first reaction to the retirement story was one of regret over the way the news broke, "because New York baseball writers have always been fair to Jackie."

The Dodgers' president said nothing about Robinson's obligations to the Brooklyn club, though these are real and not merely a matter of opinion.

It was the Brooklyn club that broke the color line and brought Robinson into organized baseball, over the opposition of fifteen other clubs and at least some of Brooklyn's own players. On Robinson's account, the whole Brooklyn club left the United States in 1947, going to Havana for spring training in order that Jackie might have his opportunity without interference from Jim Crow.

But for the Dodgers, the Jackie Robinson of this last decade would not have existed. The fact that he gave them full value on the field and the fact that after eleven years they sold his contract without consulting him, these do not alter the fact that everything he has he owes to the club.

Indeed, the fact that they sold him made it all the more imperative that he level with his employers. Had he remained with the Dodgers until retirement, it wouldn't have mattered particularly how and where he chose to announce his decision. It is, however, difficult to excuse a man in his position for sitting still and letting the club deal in good faith with the Giants when he was resolved to repudiate the deal.

His debt to the Dodgers had precedence over any agreement to sell a story to "Look," and with his mind already made up at the time of the trade he was in honor bound to speak up.

He didn't speak up. He implied that everything "would be all right," and there was a story published about breaking the news to his younger son, a Dodger fan who was distressed that his father would play with the Dodgers no longer. Jackie said he explained to the boy that this was the way things went in baseball, and in doing so he felt he had also explained matters satisfactorily to himself.

That's what he said less than a month ago. Now he says he was even then preparing the announcement of his retirement. The price has not been disclosed.

US "Skullduggery" Exposed by USSR

April 1957   New York

Well, the sordid truth is out, and from now on Allen Dulles will keep his snooping beak away from here if the miserable reprobate knows what's good for him. He and his whole Central Intelligence Agency might as well be told right out what they can do with their flamin' cloaks and daggers.

A Russian periodical called "Literary Gazette" has revealed that when we were all in Melborne for the Olympics last fall, Dulles had a stable of shapely dolls on call to corrupt the Soviet athletes.

How about that for discrimination? Our own agents skulking around Olympic Village plying Bolsheviks named Tcherniavski and Bachlykov with dainty viands and toothsome blondes, and who consoles the flower of the loyal American press along Finders and Swanston Streets? Avery Brundage, that's who. As they say Down Under, well ecktually!

It's all clear enough now that "Literary Gazette" has blown the whistle, but it is humiliating to realize that scores of the busiest ferrets in American journalism could be on the scene and fail to see what was going on under their twitching noses.

A fellow thinks back to Olympic Village now and recalls scenes in the Recreation Center which seemed innocent enough at the time. It was bright, airy and a generally merry place where kids of all nations frolicked in their spare time. During the day you might see Andy Stanfield, the sprinter, beating a Russian hurdler at chess. Others would be whacking a ping-pong ball around or writing letters or playing cards while the walls trembled under the impact of a rock-and-roll record.

In the evening Mrs. Earlene Brown would take over, and then the joint started jumping. Earlene was the belle of the ball, the darling of the international set. She is a jolly Negro girl out of Los Angeles, 226 tireless pounds, a smasher on the dance floor.

Not only Russians, but Afghans, Turks, Slavs and Finns learned rock-and-roll from Earlene. Who'd ever suspect that this jovial Mata Hari's dark purpose was to wean Soviet music lovers away from Tchaikovsky and Shostakovitch into the imperialist camp of Elvis Presley?

Yes, and under cover of Elvis' bawling, manly Muscovite hammer throwers would be out strolling beneath the Southern Cross, murmuring state secrets to Allen Dulles' "flopsies," to use the solicitous Australian term.

Allen must have swiped a leaf from Jim Norris' book and signed all available talent to exclusive service contracts, for downtown Melbourne after dark reminded hardly anybody of the Casbah.

It was downright pitiful to see dashing correspondents of the romantic Richard Harding Davis type languishing in the International Press Bar of the Melbourne Cricket Ground with no better way to pass the evening than a celibate game of ricki-ticky for the bartender's shillings.

Only once were traces of rouge and lipstick detected on Melbourne's sternly Puritan face. A chunk of the

70

American Navy sailed in one day about noon. Within an hour, the streets swarmed with gobs and every blessed one of them had a bit of fluff on his arm.

The Games were pretty well along when the fleet arrived. By that time, no doubt, the last Russian broadjumper had been brainwashed and Mr. Dulles had turned his delectable operatives out to pasture.

American agents, "Literary Gazette" reports, "tried to palm off 'secret documents' on our girls and boys. They tried to give them photographs of military objectives in order to convict them later of espionage." It is mortifying to realize that a lot of us saw that happening and thought it was only a cuddly camaraderie characteristic of childish games.

In the opening ceremonies, the big U.S.S.R. team followed the big U.S.A. delegation into the Stadium and the two groups lined up side by side on the infield. Pretty soon they broke ranks and mingled, indistinguishable in their white jackets except for a trace of tattle-tale gray in the Soviet uniform.

American girls took off their shoes and wiggled their toes in the grass. Men swapped lapel badges for souvenirs. American girls traded white gloves for the Soviets' red breastpocket handkerchiefs. Who could have known there was microfilm in every glove?

"Literary Gazette" says sneak thievery went on, and blames American spies. Melbourne hotel owners who applied the time-honored Kentucky Derby gouge will properly resent that. Since the days of the immortal robber, Ned Kelly, the home-grown Australian bandit has been the equal of any.

Joe Palmer Day at Belmont

September 1957   New York

In the dining room at Belmont, Joe Palmer's friends were swapping stories about him. It seemed only a little while ago that Joe was there, holding up his end of the conversation to say the very least, but the feature race this day was a handicap named in his memory and it was not the first or the second or the third so titled. If figures matter, it will be five years, come Hallowe'en, since the Herald Tribune's wonderful racing writer left an unfinished column in his typewriter.

"It keeps happening all the time," one fellow was saying, "that something comes around the track and I think, 'What a shame Joe isn't here to write about that.' For instance, I guess the two forms of animal life that he loathed most were state racing stewards and people who watered down whisky.

"Well, since he died there's been a man around who lost his license for cutting the whisky he served, and he was also a state steward. If Joe had been around to work him over—"

"That reminds me," another began, and while he told a story the others waited, with no especial patience, to get in one of their own. As the day wore on, truth did not necessarily prevail, which would have been all right with Joe Palmer.

"This department," Joe wrote, "had a reputation for unswerving truthfulness until approximately the age of seven, and would no doubt have it still except for leaving Kentucky temporarily at that age. But since then various things have happened, and now a certain admiration is felt for a well-told falsehood. This is wrong, of course, but there you are."

Belmont is a pleasant place and this was a pleasant, uncrowded day. Some millions were spent on physical improvements since last season, but the changes hardly show. To the casual eye this old cavalry post looks just about as it did when Joe temporarily shared Greentree Cottage there with John Gaver and would occasionally watch the morning works before bedtime.

Actually, the most noticeable change isn't on the course at all, but on Creedmor, the big mental hospital beyond the far turn. There've been additions there, a sky-scraper construction that gives the patients an unimpeded view of all the racing, even that on the Widener Chute. Almost certainly, Joe would have approved.

Conn McCreary dropped by to chat. He was one of Joe's favorite guys, though they were relentless adversaries at poker. The broken leg which Conn suffered this summer when a horse banged him against the starting gate has just about repaired itself.

Joe DiMaggio, an infrequent visitor, was in a box with friends, taking a somewhat more modest profit than he used to get from an afternoon at Yankee Stadium. "I only wish," he said, "that I'd do as well as I know the Yankees are doing."

At the moment the Yankees were playing the White Sox. There had been no report as to the score. They won, of course.

Sammy Renick, the little man who does television at the races, said he and DiMaggio had just paid a call in the jockeys' quarters.

"I took Joe in there a couple of years ago," Sammy said, "and one of the jocks looked up and said, 'Here comes God.' Today when he walked in, one of 'em said, 'Here comes God—with Renick.' Do you think that moves Joe up, or back?"

"A man who spends his life poking around racetracks," Joe Palmer wrote, "gets, in addition to a view of human nature which is at once more tolerant and less rosy than any indorsed by the clergy, a rather unreasonable fondness for certain places. I say unreasonable, because it does not seem to be dependent upon architectural or horticultural attractiveness, on setting, on comfort, or even on the quality or cleanliness of the racing at these places."

There were five fillies and mares in the Joe Palmer Handicap, all connected with somebody who had been Joe's friend. Jimmy Jones had two from Calumet Farm, just down the Versailles Pike from Joe's home in Lexington, Ky. These were Amoret and Beyond.

Attica was running in the silks of Kentucky's Hal Price Headley, and George B. Widener, president of Belmont in Joe's time, had Rare Treat. Jack Skirvin saddled the other, named Gay Life.

"On Joe's account," a man said, frowning at past performances, "I've got to bet Gay Life. I can't find any excuse for it here, though, and there are some awful nasty comments about his races."

The comments were justified. Gay Life ran out of speed early. Attica and Rare Treat ran Amoret down in the stretch and raced to a rousing finish, with Rare Treat the winner in a photo.

Joe's friends tore up their tickets and went downstairs for a bourbon—even those who preferred Scotch. They lifted their glasses silently.

No Crusades for Campanella

January 1958   New York

It was after dinner on a March evening in Dodgertown, the Brooklyn baseball team's tropical concentration camp at Vero Beach, Fla. A juke box was going full-blast in the big lounge where the players took their ease, talking, reading, playing cards, checkers, or pool.

"Come here," said Frank Graham Jr., who was the Dodgers' publicity director then. "Get a load of this."

He pushed open a screen door and nodded toward the rear of the administration building where the kitchen is.

"This club," he said with justifiable pride, "has the highest-paid orange juice squeezer in the world."

Sitting on a bench beneath the stars, helping the kitchen help and gabbing away thirteen to the dozen, was Roy Campanella, the most valuable player in the National League and one of the greatest catchers ever to pick a runner off second base.

The dishwasher and cooks and waiters were his pals. So were the players and coaches and newspaper men, the Pullman porters and dining-car staff and cab drivers. That's the way it always has been with the ample and amiable, cheerful and disarming gentlemen who was carried, critically injured, into Community Hospital, Glen Cove, L.I., before dawn yesterday.

In the great social contribution which baseball has made to America since 1946, Jackie Robinson was the trail blazer, the standard-bearer, the man who broke the color line, assumed the burden for his people and made good. Roy Campanella is the one who made friends.

No crusades for Campy. All he ever wanted was to live right and play ball. If he can never play again— and reports of the terrible damage suffered in an auto crash suggest that he never can—it will be a deep sorrow. He will be grateful, nevertheless, to be alive.

Campy has an uncomplicated appreciation of the good things that have happened to him, and a capacity for honest, unquestioning gratitude. If he were asked why he should be grateful for his chance in baseball—why he or any other decent person in a democracy should feel it necessary to thank anybody for letting him do what he could do superlatively—Roy would frown thoughtfully and answer something like this:

"Maybe I don't have to, but just the same I'm grateful it happened to me. I can remember when it couldn't happen."

If he comes successfully through the present crisis, everybody will be grateful.

"The thing about Campy," a fellow said one day, "he never knew he was a Negro until he went out to play ball."

That isn't quite so, of course, but it has elements of truth. Son of a white father, he grew up in a Philadelphia neighborhood that was as much white as black and the streets and schools and playgrounds where he spent his boyhood made no question of color.

When he was fifteen and good enough to become a professional, no scouts from organized baseball knocked at his door. A bid from the Bacharach Giants was more than he expected. After that, it was the Baltimore Elite

75

Giants and winter ball in Latin America, and it was a good life. Roy never asked for more until Branch Rickey offered more.

Even then, he only half-believed the chance was real. Probably full realization of the changes he was seeing didn't come until the night in Nashua, N.H., when his manager, Walter Alston, was chased out of a game and asked Campy to take charge. Alston isn't much for making speeches. Giving the nod to Campy in front of the other players, he was saying without words: "You are more than the best and smartest ball player on this club. You are a leader. These fellows respect you. They're white and you're not and it's never going to make any difference again."

For ten years, Campy has brought pleasure to millions. Fans watching him work were looking over the shoulder of an artist. It was even better at the squad games in Vero Beach, where one could get close enough to hear as well as see him. Joking with the hitters, encouraging the pitcher, he always had charge of those games.

"All right," he would tell a young pitcher in the last inning, "you're leading by five runs. Just throw hard down the middle, because even with good hitters the percentage is three to one against 'em."

"Only trouble with Newk," he said on one occasion when Don Newcombe was having indifferent success, "he don't push hisself."

Campy never hesitated to push hisself. Right now he's got millions pulling.

Cuba: Kidnapping of an Auto Racer

February 1958   Havana

It started like a musical comedy plot, but in the morgue laughter has a hollow ring. When the morning plane from Miami landed at Aeropuerto Rancho Boyeros, the steward said, "Here for the auto race? Better go

76

home. They've kidnaped Fangio and the race is off."
It seemed a feeble joke until, on arrival at Hotel
Nacional, the truth was learned.

Juan Manuel Fangio, of Argentina, five times world
champion race driver, actually had been snatched. Here
for the second annual Gran Premio de Cuba, a race he
had won last year, he was with friends in the Lincoln
Hotel when a stranger poked a gun against his ribs and
walked him away. Authorities were mortified but there
was little concern for Fangio's safety.

It was, in the opinion of most, merely an audacious
prank by the anti-Batista revolutionaries to harass the
government and mess up the big sports festival which
the race was to launch. Many believed that the kidnapers,
having won world attention by bringing off their coup
under the noses of Batista's police, would consider their
mission accomplished and release Fangio in time for
the start.

Rumors were thicker than the gulls on the sea wall
while guests of Pamela and Tony Vaughn gathered on
the terrace of their apartment in the Nacional. From
here they overlooked the start and finish of the three-
and-a-half-mile course along Havana's magnificent sea-
side boulevard, the Malecon. Preliminary races were on,
small sports cars ripping east along the twisting asphalt
avenue to make a U-turn at Parque Maceo, which is
something like Columbus Circle in New York, then west
alongside the sea wall to another turn-around beyond the
American Embassy.

Sea and sky were a glorious blue. Pleasure craft
plied the calm waters, a helicopter hung overhead, the
little cars droned past wooden bleachers set up on the
mall. Crowds lined the course, squatted on grassy
heights, watched from a grandstand built on top of a
filling station, leaned from the balconies of hotels and
apartment houses. The scene laid it over Indianapolis
like whisky over pop.

Rumors flooded in: Fangio had been sprung and was
in a hospital in a state of nervous exhaustion; Fangio
was in the hospital, all right, but he had been severely
beaten and doctors were undecided as to whether he

could race; Fangio wasn't in the hospital at all but had been turned loose in the suburb of Luyano about six miles away and was bound for the course by car.

Two o'clock, post time for the big race, came and went. By 3, the atmosphere was growing tense. The cars would need more than three hours for the 500 kilometers (about 312 miles) and dusk would begin settling about 6:15. There was rising indignation over a situation which had seemed at first to be only childishly irresponsible nonsense, a bizarre play to publicize a cause.

Suppose serious harm should come to a famous man who was also a guest from abroad?

At length it was announced that Fangio's colorful Maserati would be driven by Maurice Trintignat, of France. About 3:30 the cars lined up and were off with a snarling, stirring roar. Stirling Moss, of England, was in the lead followed closely by Masten Gregory, of the United States, then the American Carroll Shelby, Germany's Wolfgang von Trips and another American, Phil Hill. Fangio's blue job was fifteenth, then sixteenth.

The leaders held their positions into the sixth lap. Then watchers at the Nacional saw a cloud of dust rise just short of the embassy building. Then crowds were running, spilling onto the course, and red flags at the finish line were waving the field to a halt.

A car driven by Cuba's Armando Garcia Cifuentes had gone out of control and plowed a path through spectators on a little plot of grass called Fourth of July Park. (This, incidentally, happened on Feb. 24, which is Cuba's Independence Day.) Four men were dead and many persons injured. The death toll has risen since then to six, with 31 still in hospitals. Sirens wailed. Tony Vaughn ordered all available rooms in the Nacional made ready for victims if necessary. The race was declared over, to the approval of the drivers who complained that oil and rubber left by the preliminary races had rendered the course hazardous.

Black tragedy erased the memory of fun. Havana waited nervously for word of Fangio. It arrived shortly after midnight when he was released from a car near the Argentine Embassy.

His captors, he said, had treated him with courtesy and consideration, apologizing for what they were doing but explaining it was necessary for the good of their cause. He had been taken from his hotel to a private residence, then to another and then to a third where he slept alone and comfortably, was served breakfast in bed, declined an invitation to hear the race described by radio, did look in on television after the accident.

He isn't sore at anybody, says that if he, a foreigner, has been of service to a cause, then he is gratified.

As for the "sport" of auto racing, it should be permitted only in cages.

Man You Listen To—Phil Rizzuto

May 1958   New York

A runner on first base broke for second and was thrown out by Lawrence Peter Berra. "I wonder," Red Barber said on the air, musing, "if that was an all-out attempt to steal. Looked as if somebody might've missed a sign." He put it up to Phil Rizzuto, who concurred; yes, it was altogether possible somebody had goofed.

"On a play like that," Barber asked, "what would you say the percentage would be—that is, who'd be more likely to have missed the sign? The runner or the batter?"

Rizzuto reckoned it would be the batter.

"You mean that's what the percentage would be," Red said hastily. "You're not saying that it was the batter."

"That's right," Phil said, and there must have been

at least several members of the great unseen audience who fell to wondering how fearlessly forthright a television commentary could be, how bluntly candid and four-square. If the hit-and-run is on, and the runner goes down but the batter doesn't offer at the pitch, can the matter of responsibility be a secret?

When a player did miss a sign, Red asked, was his misfeasance mentioned in the dugout? Or did the bench preserve a discreet silence so that gentle reproof might be administered privately by the lovable old manager with heart of gold?

"No sir!" Phil said emphatically. "He hears about it, and right away."

After a moment Barber returned to the subject. It was true, then, that in big league baseball signals were missed from time to time? Oh yes, Phil said. Teams usually changed their signs for each series with a different opponent and consequently the codes could get a mite confusing.

"But how can that happen?" Barber asked. "I thought the player was supposed to flash a return sign to indicate that he got the message."

"Not necessarily," Rizzuto said. "Some teams don't ask you to return the sign. Now, the Yankees, for instance—well, maybe I'd better not say that either. Let's just say some teams don't use the return sign."

So he didn't say that the Yankees' codebook omitted responses. The inning ended about this time and, obedient to the commercial, a trip was made to the refrigerator. In the interval Red must have asked a direct question, for the next voice heard was Rizzuto's.

No, Phil was saying thoughtfully, he couldn't remember an instance when he had missed a sign while he was with the Yankees. He hastened to add that he wasn't putting himself away as infallible.

"The fact is," he said, "I had to be alert. I had to be awake and watch everything. With the sort of power I had, I wasn't going to be around very long if I took to missing signs."

This, of course, is why Rizzuto was the best shortstop the Yankees ever had. He brought the physique of a boy to a man's game but he came to play, and because he couldn't hit like a DiMaggio or Keller or Henrich, he had to make up for it by employing all the gifts he did have—his speed and agility and resolution and attention and industry and intelligence.

He learned to bunt and to drag a bunt, to dart in on the slow, high bounders past the mound and race back for those pop flies that clear the infield but are too short for the outfielders to handle. He knew where to be for a relay from the outfield and where to throw the ball when he got it.

He learned all the plays and could execute them so well that even in Phil's last days as a player Casey Stengel still pointed to him as an example for rookies who thought they were ready for the major league.

"We had to wait eight years for Rizzuto to give up," Casey said this spring, explaining why he had employed Gil McDougald so long at third base and second before assigning him to shortstop.

The fact that Rizzuto is rich in knowledge and can share it with the fans is his greatest asset on the air. Barber draws him out skillfully when they work together and their little chats are agreeably instructive, filling in gaps in the action, heightening the entertainment.

A commentator who paraded his knowledge, struck a pose as an expert, lectured his audience or second-guessed the actors—a fellow like that could be pretty obnoxious on the air. Phil just tosses in pleasant little bits. For example, the pitcher asks the umpire for a new ball and Phil remarks that pitchers have educated fingers which can discern small differences between baseballs, discovering whether the seams are perfectly even, the cover as snug as it should be, and so on.

It does not follow that a man must have excelled in sports in order to excel as a sportscaster or sports writer, nor that anybody who was good at a game can describe the game well. It does seem here, however, that Rizzuto offers an outstanding example of the simple truth that, when other things are equal, the man you listen to is the man who knows what he's talking about.

Hutch Sticks His Neck Out For Stan Musial

France and Algeria heaved in ferment, South Americans chucked rocks at the goodwill ambassador from the United States, Sputnik III thrust its nose into the pathless realms of space—and the attention of some millions of baseball fans was concentrated on a grown man in flannel rompers swinging a stick on a Chicago playground called Wrigley Field.

Warren Giles, president of the National League, had come down from Milwaukee to sit in the stands and watch Stan Musial make his 3,000th hit against major-league pitching. When the event came to pass, the game would be halted. Giles would walk out on the field to congratulate Musial with full benefit of Kodak and formally present to him the ball he had struck—if it could be found. Then the Cubs and Cardinals would return to their play.

On his first time at bat, Musial made his 2,999th hit. He got no more that day. There were still only seven men in history who had made 3,000. To be sure, there were only eight who had made 2,999, but nobody thought of that. Giles left town.

"I'll do it tomorrow," Stan said, but just before dinner the Cardinals' manager, Fred Hutchinson, phoned Jim Toomey, the club publicity man, and asked him to notify the press that Musial wouldn't start the next day's game. Unless he were needed as a pinch-batter, Hutch would let him wait until the following evening to try for the big one before a home crowd in St. Louis.

At dinner, Toomey and the newspaper men and the club secretary, Leo Ward, talked about it. Musial hadn't asked to be held out the next day. Nobody in the St. Louis office had suggested it. It was Hutchinson's own idea, prompted by his respect and affection for Musial and his realization that Stan would derive a special satisfaction out of attaining his goal in the park where he had grown to greatness.

"Maybe I'm speaking out of turn," said Bill Heinz, who was there on a magazine assignment, "but it seems to me Hutch is sticking his neck out. His team got off to a horrible start and now it's on a winning streak and he's got a championship game to play tomorrow, without his best man because of personal considerations.

"Not that the guy hasn't earned special consideration, but from a competitive point of view I think it's wrong. If the Cardinals lose tomorrow, Hutch will be blasted. He'll be accused of giving less than his best to win and it will be said the club rigged this deliberately for the box office, gambling a game away to build up a big home crowd."

"You're absolutely right," another said. "I've been thinking the same thing and I'm glad somebody agrees."

They talked it over but didn't mention it to Hutchinson. He's the manager. He must have known what he was doing.

Now it was the next day and Musial was sunning himself in the bullpen and the Cubs were leading, 3 to 1. Gene Green, a rookie outfielder, was on second base. It was a spot for a pinch-batter. Hutch beckoned.

Musial hit the sixth pitch to leftfield for two bases, scoring Green. The game stopped, Hutchinson walked out to second and shook hands. Frank Dascoli, umpiring at third base, got the ball when it was returned from the outfield and gave it to Musial. Eight cameras fired away.

You don't see that often. They don't stop games in the major leagues and let photographers invade the playing field to celebrate individual accomplishment. Baseball is as ceremonious as a Graustarkian court, but they butter the Golden Bantam before the game, not during play. Maybe this sort of thing has been done before, but not in thirty years of first-hand observation.

When the last picture was taken, Hutchinson called for a runner and Musial left the game. The manager was sticking his neck out again. The score was still 3 to 2 against the Cardinals and Musial's bat might still be needed to win, but Hutchinson took him out. It could be that Hutch lost sight of the score in the theatrics of the moment. It is no discredit to him if, just for that little while, the personal triumph of one great man meant more to the manager than team success.

As it turned out, the Cardinals kept the rally going and won the game. The next night Musial got his 21-guns from the fans in St. Louis, and on his first time at bat acknowledged the salute by flogging one over the pavilion in right.

So everything worked out happily. The way it happened was theatrical but it wasn't staged. There was nothing planned, nothing tawdry, no pre-arranged billing to disfigure the simple reality. Stan got his hit in honest competition, and it helped his team win.

Like anybody else, Musial relishes personal success and takes pleasure in the honors he wears so gracefully. Above all, though, he's a ball player in a team game, and the object is to win. Circumstances saved his greatest moment from the carnival vulgarity that would have debased it. That was good for baseball, good for the Cardinals, good for Hutchinson, and good for The Man.

Who's a Stooge? Frick! says Happy Chandler

June 1958   New York

Mr. A. Benny Chandler, a swashbuckling amphibian revered by Kentucky game wardens as The Duckslayer of Versailles, recently delivered himself of a wonderfully detached, unbiased disquisition on the present state of baseball. The game is going to hell in a handbasket, he said, because Ford C. Frick is a "puppet commissioner" and a "stooge" for the club owners.

Viewing the scene through the unprejudiced eyes of baseball's greatest living ex-commissioner, he said things were different in his and Judge Landis' day when the commissioner was a "representative of the players" and a "regulatory agency over the owners."

Mr. Chandler did history a service by disclosing this hitherto undiscovered similarity between Judge Landis and himself. If he had permitted false modesty to keep him silent, the world might never have appreciated his contributions to the game. Fans might have remembered only that as champion of the underdog and advocate for the hired hands, he defended Leo Durocher, then manager of the Dodgers, by firing him out of baseball for a year.

This was to protect Leo from the wrath of Larry McPhail, then president of the Yankees, who had been offended by a remark dropped by Durocher in Cuba. McPhail had also got Chandler his job as commissioner.

Fans are also aware that Chandler operated so effectively as a regulatory agency over the owners that the owners marked him incompetent and kicked him, bawling for just one more chance, into the street. It might never have been realized what a loss this was to baseball if Mr. Chandler hadn't set the record straight.

The disinterested and unjaundiced critic from Kentucky is not the only one to hang the tag of "puppet" on his successor. It has, indeed, become a convention to describe Ford Frick as a figurehead of impotence, a marionette manipulated by his employers.

That particular bill of goods never has sold here. This is not going to be any spread-eagle argument for the defense. There have been many occasions when it was not possible to see eye to eye with the commissioner and there will be similar cases in the future. It seems only fair, however—especially in view of the cudgeling he has received—to say that in this book Ford Frick is an able and conscientious administrator of unquestionable integrity who does his job with quiet efficiency.

Indeed, it is his insistence on doing the job quietly that gives rise to the notion that he is a messenger boy. No strutting mountebank or preening politician, he is dead set against ballyhoo for himself or his office. The investigations he conducts and the decisions he makes are seldom if ever advertised. Because there is so little publicity about the work he does, he is put away as a do-nothing.

Frick has never bracketed himself with Judge Landis or, praise be, any other commissioner. He never, never sings "Gold Mine in the Sky," even in the shower. Neither will he turn away any ball player with a grievance, and the chances are the ball players know it. For instance, when Billy Loes was fined and suspended for temper tantrums the other day, he declared immediately that he was "going to see the commissioner." If he does he'll get a hearing, though it probably ought to be in Juvenile Court.

Whenever something occurs to put baseball in an unfavorable light, somebody is quick to say, "The commissioner should have anticipated this," or "Judge Landis would never have stood for it."

On some occasions that may be so, for Frick has never pretended to infallibility, but often the affair is strictly a league or club matter in which the commissioner cannot properly interfere. Abuse of authority comes less readily to Frick's hand than it did to Landis.

When the owner of the Boston Braves broached a plan to run dog racing in his park, Judge Landis had no right to order him out of baseball, but he did. Bing Crosby, then active in California racing, was interested in buying the franchise at that time, but the judge roared, "Do you think I'm going to swap Suffolk Downs for Del Mar?"

Those were different times, maybe better, maybe not, but different. Today nobody in baseball deems it proper to tell any man how to run his business, though some run theirs very badly. Sometimes one could wish that Frick did take a firmer hand, yet in most cases it is difficult to see what he could have done in the circumstances.

This year's adventures in southern California have not been altogether edifying. The National League's abject surrender in New York was a dreadful mistake. Unblushing pursuit of profit has done baseball irreparable harm everywhere.

Still, if Frick had foreseen all the consequences, he could only have counseled against the mistakes. It is doubtful that Judge Landis could have done more with the headstrong men who are in the saddle today, and nobody ever called him a puppet.

Pity the Poor Umpire II . . . The Bean Ball

June 1958   New York

Gold, silver and bronze foundries of the land operated double shifts over the week end striking off suitable medals for the first umpires to display the red, raw courage to enforce the major leagues' new beanball rule. Up to now no blue-jacketed paunch has been decorated for valor, but we can look forward to some stirring scenes as soon as the strike zone Hawkshaws have had time to brush up on their mind-reading.

Apparently baseball was left, like Alexander, with no new worlds to conquer after Walter O'Malley met and defeated the forces of darkness on a hilly goat pasture called Chavez Ravine. Pining to open up frontiers of their own, Will Harridge and Warren Giles, presidents of the American and National Leagues, turned their attentions forthwith to the deplorable practice of skipping fast balls off the skulls of batsmen.

Hereafter, they decreed, any pitcher who throws at a batter on purpose, automatically becomes liable to a $50 fine. If he persists in his unneighborly attitude, a severer penalty will be imposed.

The task of divining the pitcher's intentions is assigned to the umpire, who has trouble enough deciding where the pitch goes, let alone why. This may be a mistake. Perhaps the job should have been turned over to Dr. J. B. Rhine, the authority on extra-sensory perception who occupies the Chair of Mind-reading at Duke University.

Announcement of the new regulations appeared in the morning papers last Saturday and perhaps escaped the umpires' attention if they happened to be concentrating that day on the past performances of Tim Tam and Cavan. This may account for the fact that although there must have been some wild pitches delivered over the week end, none was priced at $50.

Surely it cannot be that baseball's house dicks are unsure of their ability to plumb the depths of any pitcher's soul, to see and interpret the innermost workings of his psyche. Directing the umpires to distinguish between the accidental wild pitch and the intentional duster, the Messrs. Harridge and Giles are crediting them with omniscience worthy of a Broadway gossip columnist, a lofty compliment.

Not exactly going out of their way to make the job easier, the league presidents have instructed the umpires to consider the degree of wildness and the wisdom of the pitching tactics as well as the matter of intent. That is, Giles and Harridge emphasized that it was not their purpose to deny a pitcher the right to brush the batter back and loosen him up.

"Our regulations," they wrote, "are not intended to interfere with accepted pitching practices which are now and have been accepted for many years, but the intentional throwing at batters must stop."

The term, "accepted pitching practices," means the brush-back pitch. You get two strikes on the hitter, then you nudge him back a trifle with an inside pitch, then come through with the curve or fog the hard one across the outside corner. This is the classic pattern, as rigidly formalized as the minuet.

Under the new edict, umpires are not to obstruct this strategy. The batter may suspect the waste pitch is coming, may even invite it by crowding the plate, and may seek to dramatize it by flinging himself backward in exaggerated terror. The umpire is not to be deceived. "Get up, you bum," he says, "wanta live forever?"

Suppose, however, that the pitch is a half inch farther inside. Is this due to faulty control or misanthropy? "Ball one," says the believer in man's essential humanity. "Fifty bucks," says the skeptic. These are the questions that try men's souls.

Rewriting the beanball regulations, Giles and Harridge erect no sign posts to guide their deputies on the field. On the contrary, they warned them that the evidence of their eyes can be misleading.

"We recognize fully," the law givers concede, "that many incidents which may appear to be the result of intent are definitely unintentional. Many of these entirely unintentional incidents have been dramatized out of all proportion."

They're correct in that last statement, anyhow. Today's crop of baseball players, fans and writers seem to get much more hotly exercised about knock-down pitches than their elders did. Maybe this is the erroneous memory of an old curmudgeon, but it is the impression here that a good hitter of 25 years ago went to the plate expecting to hit the dirt—and he wore no protective helmet.

He got annoyed, of course, and sometimes he resorted to reprisals. But it was not then a tacit rule that a pitcher with shaky control must always be wild, low and outside, never high and inside.

There is a line so fine as to be almost indistinguishable between the viciously callous and the coldly competent. When Luke Easter played in the American League, he confessed that the pitcher who gave him more trouble than any other was that estimable aborigine, Mr. Allie Reynolds, of the Yankees. Asked why, he replied in a tone more respectful than resentful.

"He throws too hard," Luke said, "and too close."

Army's Red Blaik . . . That "Scandal" Bungle

January 1959   New York

When West Point's football team was wiped out in
that carnival of brassbound stupidity, military buckpass-
ing and bureaucratic bungling which was erroneously
called a "cribbing scandal," Red Blaik wanted more
than anything else in the world to chuck his job into
the Hudson. He wasn't merely discouraged, as any coach
might be, at the prospect of starting all over without the
fine football material that his organization had assembled and that he had trained painstakingly.

He was passionately on the side of the kids. He did
not try to conceal or condone the mistakes they had
made but he defended them fiercely as boys of good
character and he resented bitterly the slur upon their
honor. They were, he felt, at least as much sinned
against as sinning, and he knew of no other way to make
his position clear than to leave the academy with them.

In his distress, he consulted the man he has respected
above all others, his old boss, Gen. Douglas MacArthur.

"Don't quit under fire," the general said, and the
colonel said, "Very good, sir."

He stayed on the job and gave it his best, and there
never was anything better than that. Now the job is done,
and he has resigned. It is as simple as that. He gave all

of himself that the job demanded, and it demanded a great deal, and he got it done, and now he is free.

Because he dedicated himself to football without reservations, Earl Blaik understands better than most what the pressures of big-time coaching are. When his younger son, Bob, went into coaching, Red didn't actively oppose him, but he would have preferred that the boy—an honor graduate in physics at Colorado—employ his talents otherwise.

"You can put the same amount of endeavor into something else," he said, not to Bob but to friends, "and, from a selfish standpoint, be infinitely better off. It's a rarity when an individual can take successive years of the pressure of this sort of thing."

He took more years of it than most. As far back as 1933 when he was an assistant at Army, he was keenly aware of the heartburn. Army played Illinois that year, and on the field before the game Blaik encountered Illinois' realistic little Bob Zuppke. Red mentioned the nervousness he felt.

"I'm burning up inside," Zup said. "If I weren't I'd have been out of this game long ago."

Blaik will miss football for a time, but there will be compensations. "Now," he said, "I won't have to expose myself to that cold November air." There'll be other things he won't have to be exposed to, as another coach named Clipper Smith noted some years ago.

Clipper was a lot like Red Blaik in the sense that he, too, was a perfectionist who drove himself without mercy. He coached for a long time, in college and among the pros, on the West Coast and the East, before retiring to a job in industry.

"How do you feel now on Saturday afternoons?" he was asked. "Do you miss it badly?"

"I did at first," he said, "but after a while—well, you can't imagine how it feels not to have to sit still and watch an 18-year-old kid run out on that field with your salary check fluttering between his fingers."

No doubt it's corny, but it is also entirely true that if Red Blaik misses football for a while, football will miss him a great deal longer. He is a great coach, he has been a symbol of decency especially to the young men he helped grow up, and there never was a man more faithful to his principles or his friends.

He is not an easy man to know. Those who do know him are utterly devoted to him.

Big A Opens . . . Gov. Rockefeller Attends

September 1959   New York

Punctually at 11:45 a.m. yesterday George F. Seuffert upped with his baton, and the strains of the National Anthem spilled over the sunny landscape of Queens County, officially designating America's newest, biggest and gaudiest gambling hell as the land of the free and the home of the brave. For the remainder of a golden autumn day, horse players prowled the premises of New Aqueduct in a brave quest for something free. They found it—misinformation.

The "change" board at Aqueduct is an electrified gismo on top of the tote board which flashes messages in golden lights reading: "Scratch 1A," "No. 7 five pounds over," "Please bet early." Showing admirable restraint, management refrained from adding "and often."

As a matter of fact, the exhortation wasn't necessary. Unfamiliar though they were with the geography of the sprawling plant, distracted as right-thinking people must be when surrounded by 16 bars and 46 oases offering other refreshments, opening-day crowds relied on the animal instinct of the horse player and found their unerring way to the mutuel windows. There they yielded up their worldly goods as though it were their valorous aim to restore in a single afternoon the $33,000,000 spent to construct this great, glittering, gilded fleshpot. Home of the brave, indeed.

At 12:01 p.m. Gov. Nelson Rockefeller, Mayor Robert Wagner and five assistant pants-cutters assumed a Matt Dillon stance at the finish line, drew seven pairs of gold-plated scissors, and snipped a red-white-and-blue ribbon stretched across the track. Having thus cleared the way for the horses, they repaired to the Man o' War Room, the clubhouse restaurant, to break Zweiback with a thousand or so other V.I.P.s of assorted sexes.

Most of the guests wore lapel pins on which appeared a large block "A," similar to that worn by Hester Prynne.

Pains were taken to make sure that none of the 42,473 voters present would be deprived of an opportunity to view the distinguished father-in-law of Anne Marie Rasmussen in the flesh, or rather, in double-breasted worsted. The Governor broke away from the festive board in time to present a piece of hardware to the winning owner in the first race, then clasped hands over his head and strode about the paddock in front of the stands gesticulating like a victorious pug in Sunnyside Gardens. Some spectators were so unfeeling as to boo.

"They did?" said Eddie Arcaro incredulously when this was reported to him. Mr. Arcaro feels that his copyright is infringed when New York race crowds boo anybody else, but he was already under the stands, groping through the catacombs to the jockeys' quarters, when the Governor was saluted. His horse had finished out of the money in the first race.

"I got off to a great start," Eddie said wryly. "Dropped my stick leaving the gate."

"I," said Hank Moreno, "am the first jockey shut off at New Aqueduct." He, too, was out of the money, while Willie Shoemaker drove a chestnut gelding named Four Lane down the long brown stretch to win by half a length.

The first winner was an even-money favorite but Shoemaker's mount in the second race, Ira Eaker, was $9.10 and when Willie got him home in front, too, he wrapped up a $22 daily double.

Before the afternoon was done, however, Shoemaker was in a hospital with bruises, lacerations, contusions and perhaps a cracked rib. Riding Amber Morn over the turf course in the fifth race, he was thrown when his horse stumbled midway of the backstretch.

Willie's remaining assignments were canceled, of

course. Two other jockeys, Dave Erb and Bobby Ussery, gave up mounts during the afternoon, not because they were hurt but because they couldn't make the weight. They said the new steam room wasn't hot enough.

"It's a 1959 race track," one rider said mildly, "and the jocks are out doing road work like in 1900."

There were a dozen horses in the Aqueduct Handicap, the featured seventh, and Hillsdale, biggest moneywinner of the year, knocked off the winner's share of $37,880 about as expected. Carrying a tall jockey named Thomas Barrow and enough lead to make top weight of 132 pounds, the handicap star held the rail fairly close to the pace to the top of the stretch, got out of a tight fit there to come outside and win by threequarters of a length from Bald Eagle.

This time George D. Widener made the presentation, without audible objection. A lot of customers were still preoccupied trying to find their way around. Ordinarily the remarks most frequently heard at the grandstand rail are, "I shoulda had 'im," and "Whaddaya know?" But not yesterday.

At Aqueduct the password was: "I been right here alla time. Where was you?"

Leave Us Defense Against Solecisms

January 1960   New York

It was resolved on New Year's Day to make no New Year's resolutions whatever, but this doesn't rule out suggestions on how other sinners might grow in grace during 1960. It is therefore proposed that during the next 12 months all sports reporters, including those who write for the papers and especially those who broadcast by radio and television, undertake the revolutionary experiment of delivering their reports in English.

To be sure this might startle and confuse some of the clientele, yet 1960 would be a better and brighter year if we could get through it without being advised that the Syracuse University football team, say, has an attack which is difficult to "defense against."

Most of the world's sweeping reforms had small beginnings. If we could start by eliminating the barbaric and indefensible use of "defense" as a verb, there might come a day when descriptions of football games didn't twitch, quiver and crawl with such linguistic garbage as "red-dogging," "jitterbugging," "blitzing," "stunting," "look-in pass," and bastard nouns like the "keep," the "take" and the "give."

It is, of course, idle to dream of tuning in a baseball game and discovering that instead of pumping and dealing, the pitcher is winding up and throwing.

Murder of the mother tongue is a form of matricide committed with premeditation by football coaches and encouraged by writers and broadcasters as accessories after the fact.

The coachly clan enjoys pretending that butting heads is a science bordering on the occult. Hoping to bewilder and fend off the administration, faculty and alumni, the brothers shroud their sweaty craft in mystery to create the impression that football is an art so involved and technical, so profound, abstruse and esoteric as to be removed from ordinary knowledge and understanding.

It was either an illiterate coach or a sly one who misbegot the infinitive "to defense." Maybe he never learned the difference between a noun and a verb, but more likely the corruption was intentional; probably he chose to talk about "defensing the slot-T" because if he were to speak simply about stopping a play it would sound too easy.

Most professions and clans, of course, have their own special language. The medical profession talks one tongue and Madison Ave. another. These private tongues serve as a sort of stockade, giving insiders the cozy sense of belonging, mystifying outsiders and keeping them outside.

Being thrown into contact with coaches corrupts the language of reporters. Eager to crash the inner circle and eagerer to prove themselves in the know, they borrow the coachly barbarisms and employ them in tones of arrogant authority.

This establishes them as experts, at frightful cost to readers and listeners. They prattle knowingly of splits and gaps and flankers and corner-men, of options and pitches and drawers and traps, of flare passes and swing passes and buttonhook patterns and—may the Curse of Heffelfinger shrivel their busy tongues—of "loaf-of-bread passes."

During the regular season the torture has its limits, for as a rule there is only one televised college game on a Saturday, with one pro game Sunday if the local team is on the road.

Then the holiday season comes along, and the senses take a horrid clobbering. Even the man who arises feeling fit on New Year's Day, if such there be, is reduced to gibbering idiocy before the first quarter ends in the Rose Bowl.

On the first day of this year, happily, an antidote was administered. Rather, it was on the first night of this year, when the afternoon diet of football had ended and the fights came on from Madison Square Garden.

Viewers caught the last round of the semi-final between Shotgun Warner and Lee Williams. They saw Williams daze his man with heavy blows to the head, though apparently Warner had taken a substantial lead on points in the early rounds.

"We're awaiting the decision for Lee Williams over Don Warner," Jimmy Powers said cheerily, whereupon the judges split three ways for a draw. A little later the Tom McNeeley-George Logan bout was stopped and Johnny Addie took the mike.

"Logan," he said, "suffered two badly cuts over the left eyebrow."

Fans went off to bed as happy as crickets.

Debauchery and Tennis

January 1960   New York

Surrendering his gavel as president of the United States Lawn Tennis Association, Mr. Victor Denny, of Seattle, speaks out in ringing terms against debauching amateur tennis players in broad daylight. He and his colleagues in the American racquet hierarchy are unalterably opposed to a French proposal to create a class of "authorized players"—that is, players authorized to accept openly by check the wages they now receive secretly in unmarked currency.

In an essay for the publication, "World Tennis," Mr. Denny declares:

"Some of those who favor the French plan have said we should do away with 'hypocrisy' regarding amateurism, but I know of no worse hypocrite than one who would call a professional an authorized player."

The retiring president then accepted a silver pickle dish presented in appreciation of his services to the sport, which have been admirable. As to his services to Aristotelian logic, more could be said for them if he had edited that statement to read: "I know of no worse hypocrite than one who would call a professional an amateur."

According to reliable historians, Maj. Walter Clopton Wingfield was only trying to liven up a sticky garden party in Wales one afternoon in 1873 when he introduced guests to a game of his invention called Sphairistike.

He could have got the same effect, and would have been much wiser, had he merely spiked the tea with gin. For although the name of the game died peacefully soon after that fateful day, the pastime survived as "lawn tennis" to spawn more sham, deceit, trickery and downright dishonesty than any other sweaty endeavor this side of professional rassling and college football.

The origin of the term "tennis bum" is lost in antiquity but the bum is still with us, bronzed and muscular and well-scrubbed and, depending on the caliber of his forehand drive and his business acumen, more or less prosperous.

Nobody seriously pretends that a young man in moderate financial circumstances can live all his young manhood on the playground without cheating on the rules that limit his recompense to daily expenses. Why, then, cling grimly to unenforceable rules?

There is a temptation to say that the only honest men in championship tennis are Jack Kramer and the players he corrupts with legal contracts and certified checks. This wouldn't be true, though. The beautiful dreamers of the U.S.L.T.A. are honest; it's the gods they worship that are false.

With a blind devotion that sometimes seems touching, these dear old fellows genuflect before their discredited idols. They truly believe that it is nobler for an amateur to take money on the sly and lie about it than to accept pay openly and be branded a professional.

This attitude grows more ridiculous as ancient prejudices against professionalism abate. Even among the tennis fathers, scarcely anybody today clings to the superstition that professionals are unclean and that amateurs who consort with them risk some obscurely loathsome infection. After dragging their feet for twenty-five years, authorities have come around to accept the idea of open tournaments and it now appears possible that pros and amateurs will be competing on the same courts next year.

Yet they cannot face up to reality and abandon the myth of amateurism on the levels where it is an acknowledged myth.

To create a class of "qualified" players, says the U.S. L.T.A., would make a mockery of the distinction between amateurs and professionals. Of course it would, if the distinction weren't a mockery already.

That is the weakness of the French plan. Though it appears on the surface to be a step away from hypocrisy and toward a healthy candor, it is only half-a-step and the term "qualified" is only half-candid. A "qualified" player would be a paid player, and a paid player is a professional.

Why write another meaningless distinction into the language? Why not call them pros and honor them as such?

The Climate of Crime is about to be Routed

February 1960   New York

Science has at last discovered how to extract the gift of larceny from the human bosom, rendering all men as chastely virtuous as Little Eva or Cus D'Amato or Lydia E. Pinkham. No doubt this news will gratify the clergy and other guardians of the public morals such as Ford C. Frick and Sen. Estes Kefauver, but one flinches from contemplating the effect upon sports when the sincerity of every fist fighter, the probity of every tout, the nobility of every football coach and the purity of every tennis bum are all above suspicion.

A while back, a newspaper clipping was received in the mail from Mr. Leo Markson, of Elmira, N.Y. It read as follows:

"Ionization and motivation research hold promising results for cutting crime rates for stores, S. J. Curtis, security superintendent, J. L. Hudson Company, Detroit, told the National Retail Merchants' Association controllers' congress.

" 'We can't control crime any more by just locking up criminals,' he declared. 'We have to take a new approach.'

"He displayed an ionizing machine for negatively charging the air. It was about the size and shape of a desk lamp. Basing his remarks on studies showing an increase in store and other crimes when the air is positively charged, Mr. Curtis advocated converting store atmosphere so that it would be negatively ionized."

It has, of course, been common knowledge for a long time that there is such a phenomenon as a climate of crime, an atmosphere of sin. Few of us are too young to remember when boxing and basketball used to fill Madison Square Garden and you could walk into the lobby and literally feel corruption in the air.

Only now do we discover what caused this. It wasn't heredity or environment that made Jake LaMotta the way he was. It was too many positive ions in the atmosphere.

The new knowledge offers a happy alternative to Sen. Kefauver's investigation of boxing, Congressional and Senatorial inquiries into baseball, the numberless and interminable hearings and trials of Cus D'Amato, and the whispered questions about Baltimore money is showing on the Colts plus 6½.

No longer will it be necessary to stir up the dying embers under Frankie Carbo or hire former G-men to dog the footsteps of stars in the National Football League. A little gimmick, the size and shape of a desk lamp, will drain dishonesty from the atmosphere and render every competition pure as puppy love—with a 12-month, money-back warranty from General Electric or Westinghouse.

It is easy to conjure up—hell, it's impossible not to imagine—what a scrubbed and beamish face sports will present to the world in the bright ionized world of tomorrow. Let us picture a dugout in the Continental League, occupied by a team under the management of Leo Durocher, a brand that Branch Rickey will have snatched once more from the burning.

The Minnie-Paul Saints, generally identified in headlines as the St. Leos in the interest of brevity, are leading by one run but the Dallas Fts. have a man on third base and their leading hitter, Smead Jolley III, is at bat. The pitcher for the Saints, just out of junior high and understandably nervous before a crowd of almost 400, glances toward the dugout for advice.

His manager is sitting next to the water cooler, removed as far as possible from the ionizing machine. He cups hands to his mouth, and in the tense hush his voice seems to fill the park:

"Stick it in his ear!"

For an instant there is shocked silence on the Saints' bench. Then a gasp of scandalized dismay.

100

"Leo!" says Eddie Stanky, the third base coach, "why, Leo! We're surprised!"

The doughty little manager is blushing to the roots of his—well, the hair is gone but the roots remain.

"Gracious, fellows," he mumbles, "I'm sorry. I—I guess I just forgot myself. I—I—Eddie, you take the team, will you please, like a good chap?"

Covered with pretty confusion, he gropes back to the clubhouse to wash out his mouth with ionized soap.

North Disneyland: the Winter Olympics

February 1960   Squaw Valley

Ten inches of fresh snow, delivered on order of Mickey Mouse's all-powerful creator, came swirling out of the general direction of Hollywood into this notch in the high Sierras today, converting yesterday's muddy hogwallow into North Disneyland. Because nothing is impossible for Mr. Walt Disney, the pageantry which he designed to open the VIII winter Olympics had a stage setting as extravagantly theatrical as man and nature could devise for the noble pastime of sliding down hill.

Highways that were dry yesterday turned soft and tricky as cars crept into a clotted snarl near the valley's narrow mouth, swinging their sterns like starlets on parade. After five years of scheming and feuding, politicking and panhandling and frantic building, there was a fifteen-minute delay before cannon boomed at the base of Papoose Peak, American, Greek and Olympic flags were hoisted, and the international coasting carnival was under way.

Falling snow curtained the valley in heavy gray as the crowds trudged in from the parking lots, gasping and blowing at an altitude of 6,200 feet. Then, as though on signal from Mr. Disney himself, the blizzard was shut off and the sun came out at the instant the ceremonies began.

The first day included nothing rash or impetuous like

competition, just made-in-Hollywood spectacle, the some-times abominable snowmen from thirty nations, plus their generally delectable dolls, came trudging over from the Olympic Village in their overshoes, paraded around the outdoor speed-skating oval, marched into the three-walled ice arena past the "tribune of honor" where Vice-President Richard M. Nixon stood, and deployed by teams in the big hall.

Because the summer Olympics originated in Greece, protocol demands that Greece lead these processions, even though Greeks are smart enough to stay out of the cold and have no winter sports team. For a while the brass contemplated an alphabetical lineup led by a skiing squaw from Argentina but at the eleventh hour succor arrived for tradition.

A Greek travel agent from San Francisco, name of George Hatzis, showed up to carry Greece's standard at the head of the parade. By his own confession, George takes no part in winter sports, but he clomped along erect and dutiful, displaying a modest bay window under the waist of his stretch-pants.

First actual athlete in the procession was a blonde squaw of provocative design, Miss Maria Cristina Schweizer, of Buenos Aires. She skis on snow and water, plays tennis, swims, yachts, speaks four languages and fills her dark green stretch-pants for a rating of 8, an al-together admirable score.

In the frostbite set, stretch-pants competition is at least as important as the giant slalom. They are de rigeur for dames, and they must not wrinkle anywhere, no mat-ter what the position or how great the strain. Here there is no official committee to rate them so the work is done by qualified ski writers.

Rating is based on conformation alone, neither breed-ing nor downhill form being taken into consideration. Theoretically, scores range from 6 to 10, those who can't make a 6 being unrated. Actually, however, no rating of 10 ever has been approved, for this is perfection known only in a ski writer's dreams.

On one noteworthy occasion, a Vermont ski coach was tried out as a judge. Though he had been in strict physical training since midsummer, always walking up and down stairs backward to strengthen his leg muscles, his knees buckled when a blonde goddess swayed past him, not a ripple showing anywhere.

Gasping, he scored her a 10, but his card was taken away from him and he was disqualified as "too emotional."

It is still too early in these games to know whether a new record will be set, but a hasty survey suggests that some of the domestic and imported squaws will rate at least 8.6 and there may be a Norwegian qualifying for a smashing 9. Even though lady discus throwers have the advantage of competing in their drawers, contestants in the summer Olympics aren't in the league with these frosted cookies.

Well, the marchers trudged in, bands played, people sang, the wheels of amateurism and politics talked into microphones, Disney-sent-up colored balloons and gunfire terrified 2,000 pigeons that were sprung out of cages.

The spectacle of these birds fluttering and circling in terror recalled last autumn's Army-Air Force game in Yankee Stadium, when the Air Force turned loose several trained falcons that chased every pigeon out of the ball park. These may have been relatives, for circling and veering they headed east down the valley, toward Yankee Stadium.

At length there was a pause, then Andrea Mead Lawrence, winner of two gold medals in 1952, came scooting down from Papoose on skis. Carrying the Olympic torch with an honor guard of ski troopers at her heels, she slid sedately, as befit the mother of four.

February 1960   Squaw Valley

Yesterday's dispatch touched upon the perplexity of a ski buff from Denver who bought a $1,000 package trip to the Winter Olympics, including a $250 loge seat in the ice arena. On the two occasions when he attended arena events, there was no gatekeeper to take the ticket.

Well, some light has been shed on this. It seems one

of the security police was led to a gate and told, "This is your station. Guard it with your life." Conscientious but confused, he planted himself in front of another door nearby and demanded credentials of all who sought to enter. The door was behind him, else he might have noticed the sign on it reading: "Gentlemen."

To sum things up on departure from this winter wonderland of Walt Disney: Squaw Valley has, in all probability, the finest winter sports facilities in the world; the carnival up to now has been blessed by incredibly glorious weather; immaculate peaks against a spotless sky shimmer in warm sunshine which makes the valley floor a slum of slush and mud; the competition has been first rate, though much of it is invisible except to a spectator who can be in a dozen places at the same time; the prices are outrageous.

For a customer who pays $7.50 to get into the valley, $2 to park and $25 for an arena seat, the daily program is a trifle thin. There aren't really enough events to fill 11 days, except for those who enjoy standing around in slush ogling the occupants of stretch pants.

A typical day starts at 8 a.m. with a cross-country race, but that's at McKinney Creek, 15 miles away. At 8:30 capitalists in the arena may watch compulsory figure-skating, in which dames do interminable figure-eights and judges squat peering at the skate tracks. At 9, dames start racing against time on the outdoor speed-skating oval, but most customers ignore that to scramble up a mountain so they can see a fragment of the Alpine ski race scheduled for 10 o'clock. That's finished by 11, and for peasants without arena tickets for the afternoon hockey, that's all except for victory ceremonies beneath the Olympic flame at 2:30 p.m.

Though it costs somewhat more than a ringside seat for Dempsey and Firpo, the hockey can be exciting. The only match scheduled today was a consolation game between Finland and Japan, non-winners. This is Japan's first Olympic hockey team, and the little rascals have achieved great popularity, losing by scores of 19 to 1 and 19 to 0.

Nippon's gallant goalie, Tochiei Honma, could face a

Castro firing squad and never know he had left Squaw Valley. In two games he crouched courageously in the net while 26 goals hummed past his ears and the puck caromed off his torso for 89 saves before he hollered copper. Then a substitute named Shoichi Tomita went in for 38 saves and 12 goals.

In the event the New York Rangers want Honma to replace injured Gump Worsley, his address is Shimeri-ryo, Kiyotaki-Tanse-cho, Nikko-ski, Tochigi-ken, Japan. He can also be reached at his parents' home, Seppu-eki mae, Niikappu-gun, Hokkaido, Japan.

There is a growing impression that the American hockey team, easily our best in the Olympics thus far, may have a chance against the Russians and Canadians. Smashing Sweden, 6 to 3, with an impetuous attack that produced four goals in the first period, they looked twice as fast and skillful as the Russians did beating Czechoslovakia, 8 to 5, on the same day.

Russia has a dandy goalie named Evgeni Erkin, a cat in the nets, and an elegant skater at right wing named Veniamin Aleksandrov, or plain Benny Alexander. For their match the Czechs wore red uniforms and the Russians white, except for Erkin, whose red shirt so disconcerted opponents that the game was stopped while he changed to white.

The game got pretty emotional, with one lively little fist fight in front of the Soviet goal. Two-minute penalties were given Russia's Alfred Kuchevski and Czechoslovakia's Miroslav Vlach. In Olympic language their infractions were defined as cross-checking and slashing. In English that means slugging.

Mention should be made of Disney's phony snow sculpture which festoons the landscape. The statues depict snowmen on skates and skis in attitudes considered humorous, and each has a printed commercial for some California city at its base. The commercials cost $2,000 each.

The statues are made of a material used for Christmas tree ornaments, which crumbles in the wind. Workmen go around patching them with tape. For emergency cases there is a statue hospital on the premises.

Fine arts are not restricted to the valley. Last night

in Nevada Lodge over on Lake Tahoe, a left-handed lady crap shooter held the dice for 45 minutes and made them send out for money three times.

The Battle of Chavez Ravine

March 1960   Los Angeles

Chavez Ravine is a topsy-turvy goat pasture close to the heart of this city, a catchall for rusty tin cans and broken bottles, with a few unimposing shacks still standing on its pock-marked landscape. For more than two years it has been the most widely publicized battlefield since Omaha Beach, but now Walter O'Malley is paying cash for peace.

Bulldozers are pushing 2,000,000 cubic yards of mud from the hilltops into the ravine. They have made pretty good progress leveling 45 acres for construction of a new playground for the Dodgers, though its appearance does not encourage the notion that the project can be completed in time for the opening of the 1961 baseball season. A fine but persistent rain over the last 24 hours has made a hideous hog-wallow of the site.

However, the muck will dry fast when sunshine ultimately cuts through the smog. Grass can be grown rapidly in this earthly paradise. And engineering plans call for the stadium to be prefabricated on the spot. That is, a plant is to be constructed to pre-cast concrete and steel sections which cranes will swing into place as fast as they are made. By this means, perhaps, the target date can be met.

Meanwhile, O'Malley's got to shell out.

Everybody is familiar with the deal giving the Dodgers' president title to 315 acres for a ball park and some rather vaguely described public recreational facilities which he agreed to maintain for 20 years. In addition to the land acquired from the Federal government—after plans for a housing development were abandoned—there

106

were privately owned parcels considered essential to the project.

The city attempted to buy these parcels at their total appraised value of $92,850, but the owners banded together to resist. They were willing to sell, but they took a fancy to a different figure—approximately half a million.

Chances are O'Malley could go to court and beat them, but this would delay the project maybe another two years, and every delay is a pang in the pocketbook for O'Malley, who is being squeezed by his present landlord, the Coliseum Commission.

This year the Commission is taking a flat 10 per cent of the gate as rent for Memorial Cow Pasture, plus all the income from concessions. This will come to about $800,000 if the Dodgers match last year's business.

Of course the Dodgers could play in Wrigley Field, the minor league park they own, but that plant can hold only a fraction of the crowds they draw in the Cow Pasture. Tossing out that alternative as unthinkable, O'Malley had the choice of being gouged by the land owners or gored by the Commission. He chose the former.

Agreements completed about ten days ago call for O'Malley to pay $494,400 for the land valued by the court at $92,850. Some of the owners have brought off deals that would do credit to the James brothers.

There's a guy named Francis Scott whose house and land were appraised at $9,000. He's getting about sixteen times that figure—$150,000. Charlotte Hanson's $8,500 parcel goes for $60,000, Francis de Leon is collecting $130,000 for two pieces, a little grocery store and a residence valued at $25,150 together.

The prices seem slightly exorbitant until it is recalled that O'Malley will wind up with 315 acres in a swiftly growing metropolis at a cost of half a million.

The development is supposed to cost $15,000,000, with the city building all the access roads. As now planned, the park will accommodate 56,000 customers. The Dodgers have $7,000,000 from the sale of Ebbet's Field and other sources, expect to borrow the remainder.

After making his original deal with city and county

officials, O'Malley had to campaign for public approval in a referendum, had to win three favorable verdicts in the California Supreme Court and another in the United States Supreme Court.

Meanwhile, he was paying rent on Ebbet's Field, paying taxes and maintenance costs on Wrigley Field, paying rent in the Coliseum, paying legal fees. Yet still the money rolls in.

The Hot Seat

December 1960   New York

The scene is the directors' room high in the tower of the Wrigley Building in Chicago. It is simply but richly furnished, with a diamond-shaped council table of polished sapodilla, flannel upholstery on the chairs, bearskin scatter-rugs and walls painted a restful spearmint green. On a window many floors above the river is a painted X marking the spot where Lou Boudreau, Charley Grimm, Bob Scheffing and predecessors as manager of the Cubs jumped, fell or were pushed.

At the head of the table sits Phil K. Wrigley, president of the Cubs, flanked by six or eight vice presidents. The next eight chairs are occupied by coaches. At the foot of the table stands a squat metal contraption with electric wires afflxed. The seat, obviously hot, is unoccupied.

(Central casting has promised to furnish players for all parts by the time this drama goes into rehearsal. At present, the only performers who have accepted roles as coaches are Rip Collins, Elvin Tappe, Vedie Himsel and Harry Craft.)

As the curtain rises, all are chewing rhythmically. The president raps briskly with a gavel.

Wrigley: The meeting will come to order. Doublemint, anyone? Mr. Collins, you're new here. That isn't, uh—that couldn't be a Topps wrapper in your pocket, surely? Good heavens! Beechnut cut plug! Ah, Mr. Holland (addressing a vice president), perhaps you'd have a little chat with Mr. Collins after the meeting? Thank you.

Wrigley (resuming after a stern silence): Now, gentlemen, you've probably guessed why I asked you here today. Possibly some of you have learned through the newspapers that we are seeking a man to occupy that empty chair down there, the right man, the best possible man.

Mr. Boudreau was the last occupant but unfortunately he is no longer with us. Mr. Grimm was here before him—for the third time, I think it was, or maybe the sixth. Not an easy man to keep track of, Mr. Grimm, an itinerant banjo player. Then there was Mr. Scheffing and, let's see . . . yes, Mr. Phil Cavaretta. Fine men all of them but none, in my judgment, the right man.

As you probably know, gentlemen, our past policy has been for the vice presidents, general managers and myself to hire a man to occupy that seat with the title of manager. He would then select four or five pinochle cronies as coaches and then I would fire him if somebody in our little family here hadn't already cut the ground from under him.

This year we're going at it differently. You coaches down there are going to choose the manager, but we're not going to call him by that title. Smacks of feudalism, in my opinion. We'll call him head coach, perhaps, or chairman of the board. First, however, a chicle break. Do try a stick, Mr. Collins. Refreshing, isn't it?

(All chew silently until the president wields the gavel again.)

Wrigley: Delicious. Amazing how the flavor lasts. Now perhaps some of you gentlemen feel that we're going about this business in an unusual fashion, even an unorthodox fashion. I should explain that this organization has always been receptive to new ideas.

Years ago when my father was in charge here, there was a sports writer on one of the papers named William Veeck, Sr., whose articles were sharply critical of the operation. I daresay no other man in baseball would have defied tradition as William Wrigley did. Instead of writing to the editor demanding that Veeck be fired, he called the young man in and said: "You know so much about how a ball club should be run, why don't you try?" "I will," Veeck said, and he got winners, too.

I had a similar experience with another newspaper-man, a chap named Jim Gallagher. He did quite well after I hired him as general manager, but I was adding vice presidents at the time and it became so crowded around here that Mr. Gallagher found himself elbowed all the way to Philadelphia.

Now then, gentlemen, are we ready? There are pencils and pads in front of all you coaches. You understand what we want. I'd like each of you to write down the name of one man, the right man, the best man. Then fold your ballots and pass them up here, if you please.

A pregnant silence falls, in which can be heard faint sounds—heavy breathing, teeth gnawing on pencils, the scratch of labored writing. Eight slips are passed to the president, who takes them to a window where they can be read, this being the only directors' room in baseball without artificial lighting.

Wrigley (muttering as he reads): Let's see, now . . . the right man . . . Collins, one vote . . . Tappe, one vote . . . Himsel, one vote . . . Craft, one—

(The curtain falls heavily.)

The Bowie Breed

January 1961   New York

Tastefully attired in wool hats and cerise-on-magenta sports shirts, a pampered band of horse players, cracker division, assembled at Hialeah yesterday for the opening of a 40-day meeting. In sunny, smoggy California, Santa Anita has been coddling the avaricious since the last week of December. In both cases, this is winter racing where it's summer, strictly for sissies.

Now comes the true test of gallant greed—winter racing where it's winter. On Saturday of this week, Bowie opens for business in the snowy thickets of Maryland. It is the earliest spring in the history of the state (last year's vernal meeting didn't begin until the dogdays of February, opening on Lincoln's Birthday).

Offering "48 golden days of sport," the backwoods kraal between Baltimore and Washington will operate five days a week through March 29, or as long as one parlay player's head is visible above the drifts. This is more than a week longer than usual, for it includes eight days snowed out in 1959.

This year Tuesdays as well as Sundays are left open, for two reasons. In the event that blizzards interrupt the entertainment, the programs frozen out can be fitted in on the open Tuesdays. Also, the five-a-week schedule allows for gambling on 10 Saturdays, traditionally the most profitable days. Mr. Don C. Lillis wouldn't be president of Bowie and senior partner in a Wall Street investment firm if he couldn't count his change.

Though Mr. Lillis' political convictions are a matter between him and his precinct leader, his choice of dates is obviously motivated by patriotism, a reponse to young Mr. Kennedy's call for a fitter America beyond the New Frontier. While Florida and California cosset the covetous to the edge of decadence, Bowie has always striven to toughen the $2 plunger. Indeed, the hardihood of the Bowie Breed is practically legendary.

Everybody remembers the gallant company, 1,000 strong, trapped overnight in the clubhouse by a Saturday blizzard two years ago. At first Gus Hartshorn, in charge of the Stevens commissary, was worried. He telephoned Joe Stevens in New York: "Mr. Joe, a terrible thing has happened—"

"Have you closed the bar?" Mr. Joe asked, putting first things first. Actually, there was no cause for alarm. Gus broke out sandwiches and coffee, and Sunday found 1,000 waifs still contentedly blowing into their fists to keep the dice warm.

In tribute to these orphans of the storm, a rather sentimental ceremony was conducted on opening day last year. Mr. Lillis imported a waddle of penguins who lined up at the clubhouse gate in their snappy thermal attire

111

and were the first clients admitted. Later these Antarctic refugees were presented to the Baltimore zoo.

Specimens of the Bowie Breed who show up Saturday will find the entire grandstand glassed-in and heated, with big ventilating blowers to clear the air round losers. Perhaps this is an improvement, yet it must be viewed with mixed feelings.

Horse players love to suffer. They are never truly happy unless they are miserable—freezing or sweltering or drenched by rain, shiny in the seat and tissue-thin in the sole, elbowed and trampled and bruised in cramped space where the air they breathe has already been breathed several times, unable to find a slat to sit on or a winner to back, stony broke and sinking hopelessly deeper into debt.

Nowhere has this design for living been honored more faithfully than at Bowie. In the old days the Maryland season always opened and closed there, with a short meeting in the raw rains of April and another among the snow flurries of late November and December.

When the spring and fall meetings were abandoned in favor of a single glorious frolic in a winter wonderland, the joint retained all its oldtime charm, perhaps even expanded it. Not only could the patron have a perfectly wretched day betting losers but a frostbitten ear might snap off to boot.

Now, well, we'll just have to wait and see. Creature comforts are all very well in the plush sinkholes of Las Vegas, but the clientele attracted by strippers and one-armed bandits has little in common with the Bowie Breed. When a horse player has nothing to complain about except the jockey's dishonesty, the trainer's incompetence, the placing judges' myopia and the stewards' indifference to fouls, he may very well quit the game cold and just stay home and beat his wife.

Attendance and mutuel figures will furnish the answer. In recent seasons Bowie has drawn an average of 12,000 to 13,000 Eskimaux daily with a handle running above $1,000,000. If the winterized plant starts attracting loafers who'll just sit around dozing in the artificial heat when

112

they ought to be tearing their pants getting to the $5
windows, Mr. Lillis will have only himself to blame.

Once a breed has been fixed, like the thoroughbred, or
schnauzer or Poland China, it's a mistake to tamper with
it.

"Lingering" Death Overtime?—No!

January 1961   New York

With two minutes to play, the New York Giants led the
Baltimore Colts, 17-14. New York had the ball on its own
25-yard line, third and four. If the Giants could make
one first down they could dawdle through at least four
more plays while the clock raced on and the professional
football championship of 1958 dropped into their laps.

Frank Gifford hit the line, was one foot short. De-
clining the gamble, New York punted. It was Baltimore's
ball 86 yards from the goal line.

Lenny Moore ran once and Johnny Unitas threw eight
times. Incomplete passes stopped the clock five times.
Once the Colts called time out. Racing the flying seconds,
they reached the Giants' 13-yard line. Steve Myhra
kicked a field goal from placement, tying the score. Nine
seconds remained, enough for a kick-off and one play
that got nothing. The gun ended the game and
started another.

Now the clock lost all meaning. Time literally stood
still. No need for haste now, for the lights were on and
time limits off and the teams could keep at it all night
until one or the other scored. With the opening of the
sudden-death fifth period, this ceased to be football
played under football rules, because the essential factor,
time, had been removed.

On the toss of a half dollar by Ron Gibbs—no two-
bit referee he—the Giants won the privilege of receiving
the kick-off. Again they failed by a foot to make first
down, chose to punt on fourth rather than try for those
12 inches. There was no hurry. All they had to do to

get the ball back was stop Baltimore, and they'd been reading all season about their defensive unit, the noblest band of heroes since Leonidas at Thermopylae.

So the Colts went 71 yards to first down on the New York 8, disdained the field goal that would have ended it there, and sent Alan Ameche in for the six points that won the championship, beat the point-spread and clobbered the handbooks.

Pro football fans still savor the memory of that finish, but now Pete Rozelle wants to paint the lily. If the National League's boy czar had his way, the Giants would be given another chance to tie the score so there could be a sixth period then—well, Pete just hates to see a season end.

At least, a game without end seemed to be the goal Rozelle had in mind when he said the other day that he would propose changes in the league's sudden-death rule, though re-reading of his suggestion corrects that first impression. Actually, he just wants to guarantee both teams one chance to score in the overtime period.

As the Commissioner sees it, it would have been unfair to the Colts if the Giants had carried the overtime kick-off back to score, thus ending the game before Baltimore could get the ball. In such an event, he'd have another kick-off, to Baltimore this time. If the Colts then lost the ball on downs, they'd be licked; if they tied the score, the whole business would start over.

What Pete wants is lingering, not sudden, death. It is devoutly hoped he doesn't get it. Overtime play is an artificial expedient at best, an unnatural device to avert a tie in a play-off for the title.

On the one occasion when the extra period was needed to decide the championship, it added to the day's excitement. It worked out equitably, too, for the Giants had their chance and muffed it and the team that deserved to win did win. But one of these in a decade is plenty. Better that one team should get the short end of the stick than let the show drag on like the death scene from "Camille."

Statistics might disprove it, but the impression here is that the pros hardly ever stop anybody. A ludicrously high proportion of games during the season are decided in the closing seconds, and the only reason for this can be incompetent defensive play. Sunday after Sunday, the last team in possession goes on to score, and if it's a close game that last score is the clincher.

Far too often, the game they play is closer to bean-bag than football, yet it could be even worse. Get a couple of those firehouse teams into an overtime match where they take turns tying the score and you know what you'd have? Basketball, that's what.

Man Who Neither Gabs nor Coos— Don Dunphy

January 1961   New York

In the eighth round Florentino Fernandez, a blown-up Cuban welterweight with a small privet hedge under his nose, fetched Rory Calhoun a baleful hook in the chops and although Calhoun didn't react instantly, Don Dunphy did. For television watchers, he called attention to the blow and suggested that Rory might suffer a delayed reaction.

Sure enough, a second or so later Calhoun's offensive operations ground to a stop. Only then, it appeared, did Fernandez realize what the commentator had spotted as the punch connected—that he had a plum ripe for pluck-ing. He got excited, as many young fighters do in the circumstances, but not so excited as to blow the op-portunity.

The Cuban stepped up his attack, missing a good deal, but connected with another good hook. Calhoun's right leg went limp and fluttery. Alerted by the announcer, the most inattentive and least informed viewer could see that he was hurt.

"Downstairs," said a man at the bar. "Go for the body, chump." But fighters seldom heed advice to their TV images. Still fishing for the head and missing often,

115

Fernandez caught his man at last with a left and right and knocked him out.

Dunphy had called it perfectly, recognizing the first punch as a good one, sensing its effectiveness, anticipating the finish. He provided just the perceptive comment needed to complement the camera, which frequently catches the punches without conveying any notion of their effect.

For years, Dunphy has ranked in this book as the best of the electronic fist-fight reporters. He was the best of a long line of radio broadcasters and when he took on the Saturday night television series he established himself as best in that field.

In radio's early years, sportscasters were comforted by the knowledge that "what they can't see won't hurt 'em." They employed dramatic license freely, knowing in those pre-transistor times that their listeners couldn't see what was going on. No matter how slow the action might be, the unforgivable sin was to bore the sponsor, and many a beau butterfly would have been enchanted to discover what a beast of prey he had seemed over the airwaves.

Now and then if you sat in the working press row near the microphone you could hear, in a hall otherwise silent with ennui, Homeric accounts of strife between gladiators who were in fact standing eight feet apart and regarding each other with tender affection.

By the time Dunphy came along the situation had improved to the point where accurate reporting was permissible as long as it didn't put the customers to sleep. The newcomer combined keen perception with simple exposition and could keep pace with the swiftest action without sacrificing clarity. It was possible to judge a fight you were hearing by radio and come pretty close to the official score.

The first television voices belonged mostly to radio announcers who had been brought to regard silence as a loathsome thing, a crime against nature. Their chatter was an infuriating distraction to a viewer trying to see for himself what was happening.

Then the pendulum swung to the other extreme and

we had a succession of effigies at the microphone whose single qualification was the ability to coo the commercials in persuasive accents. Apparently they watched the overhead clock rather than the ring, for their chief contribution to knowledge and understanding was contained in the recurrent announcement: "One minute left in the round."

Some were untrained observers, patently unable to differentiate between a jab and an uppercut, unschooled in boxing tactics. Because they didn't see what was going on and couldn't describe it, they broke silence only to read prepared material of gripping inconsequence, like a roster of southpaw bantamweights who had performed in Madison Square Garden since it moved uptown.

At least, the strong, silent type was a relief after the earache boys. "I like So-and-So," you would hear fight fans say, "because he doesn't talk too much." Obviously, if the best commentators were those who commented the least, the perfect one would be a deaf mute or a dead man.

Dunphy is the happiest medium unwrapped thus far. He doesn't burden the viewer with chatter but he seems to know what aspects of the fight may be lost in transmission and ought to be reported orally. He is timid about expressing his judgment about how the contest is shaping up. And he is, as he demonstrated the other night, quick to direct attention to the significant.

Bribes and Basketball ... Everett Case's Case

May 1961   New York

It may be that reading the paper while lying face down puts the news into a different perspective, sometimes causing pain in an unexpected area. Anyhow, there was this exercise in soul-searching by Everett Case, roundball coach at North Carolina State, whose ablest operatives have been accused of jobbing games for pay.

The dispatch from Raleigh reported that Coach Case,

"generally credited with bringing big-time basketball to the Atlantic Coast Conference area by recruiting out-of-state players 15 years ago," had decided that "New York talent" was responsible for the crookedness. Two of the State players charged with taking bribes are from Brooklyn, the third from Louisville, Ky.

"Maybe the sense of values of New York boys is all screwed up," Case said. "I don't know, but the North Carolina boys would certainly be loyal."

The poor, bewildered, unreasoning, mixed-up guy. After a lifetime in the dream-world of children's games, he has been hit in the eye by a fact and he doesn't know how to face up to it. He's got integrity confused with geography.

If the sense of values of some New York boys is screwed up, not to mention some boys from Louisville and some from Philadelphia and some from Connecticut, then the important question is how it got that way. What standards of behavior do these young men have, and where did they acquire them?

Most kids of college age are idealists. Any bona-fide undergraduate—from the sandhills of Carolina or the streets of New York or the badlands of Dakota—who goes out for the team and makes it will play as well and honestly as he can for his personal satisfaction, for the good opinion of his schoolmates and, begging Ralph Henry Barbour's pardon, "for the honor of the school." He will, as Case says, be loyal. Anything else would be unthinkable.

It is not the Hessian's fault that he is indoctrinated in a different code. Starting in his impressionable high school days, older and presumably responsible men representing reputable institutions have reminded him that he has something for sale, that his athletic skills have a cash value. "You're a chump if you don't take the best bid," the recruiters tell him, again and again.

The same men who have hammered this cynical philosophy home are shocked when the kid accepts a higher bid from some punk named, say, Aaron Wagman. They wonder where the corruption started.

Don't they realize that a boy who can be bribed to

shoot baskets can also be bribed to miss them, if the price is right?

Carolina high schools, Case says, don't produce the polished basketball players that come to college from other regions. This, he explains inferentially, is why he has gone outside the state for his material. Now he is disillusioned.

"The recruiting is too vicious," he says. "The rivalry is too vicious. We're so close together in this state, and everybody wants to win. . . . Basketball is meant to be a game. Down here it has turned into a war. I'm ready for a truce."

After 15 years, he ought to know. Yet does he? He seeks refuge and solace in the Case Law: you can take the boy out of the city but you can't take the city out of the boy. He does not seem to realize that the seeds of corruption grow as readily in red clay as in asphalt.

To repeat, maybe lying prone to read the papers gives a guy the wrong slant. Yet from this position it is difficult to discover much difference between the honest coach who hires players and the crooked gambler who tops his price.

One wants to win games and succeed in his profession. The other wants to win bets and succeed in his. One is within the law, one outside, but both make compromises with ethics and the fixer pays top dollar. No school can afford $1,000 or $1,200 a game.

Acting after the fact to fit a new padlock to the stable door, authorities of North Carolina and North Carolina State have announced a policy of "de-emphasis," setting up immigration quotas on out-of-state talent, limiting non-conference competition and putting summer leagues like those in the Borscht Circuit of the Catskills off limits. (This last taboo stems from the theory that evil flourishes in refined mountain air.)

"We were sure at the outset," said William B. Aycock, Chancellor of the University at Chapel Hill, "that the only way we could be certain there was no bribery and no scandals was to have no intercollegiate athletics."

The authorities didn't want to be that certain, though,

119

so they didn't abolish the sports program altogether. It isn't always necessary to shoot a dog in order to rid him of fleas. It just seems so sometimes.

O'Malley in a Manger

May 1961   New York

This is to acknowledge a debt to Arthur E. Patterson, press agent for the Los Angeles Dodgers, who has demonstrated once again that he is never too busy to contribute his time, wisdom and literary talent for the benefit of less gifted comrades. Recently this generous chap interrupted his crowded schedule to spell out, appraise, amplify and offer constructive criticism of certain observations made here regarding baseball in the City of Angels—and all this, mind, without even being asked.

The Yankees' first visit to the Pacific Coast in early May brought capacity crowds (up to 19,865) to Wrigley Field, the vest-pocket heaven where the Angels tread, creating the liveliest demand Southern California ticket scalpers have experienced since Aimee Semple McPherson was at the top of her game.

It was remarked then that if the Angels had been able to schedule the attraction in Memorial Coliseum (top baseball gate, 92,706 paying $552,774.77), the income would have eased the financial suffering of Gene Autry, Bob Reynolds and associates, who are investing something like $5,000,000 to get the American League started out there.

However, it was pointed out, the Dodgers' Walter O'Malley has declared the Coliseum off-limits for the Angels, even when his team is not using it. For a mere $100,000, he gave the Angels his permission to exist, but forbade them to share a playground with his team until such time as a new park would be ready in Chavez Ravine, where he will collect the rent.

This statement of fact sent Patterson to his files,

120

where he appears to have preserved a flattering number of essays clipped from this space. He quoted at length from that source to re-establish the truth that baseball in Memorial Cow Pasture is a sordid travesty, a corruption and mockery.

"Strangely," he observes, "those are the writings of a man who now advocates that not only one team but two teams should play their home games there. . . . If Coliseum baseball is a 'hoax' as Smith claims, why compound the crime by offering both NL and AL hoaxes?"

Apologies to Mr. O'Malley are in order, along with a grateful expression of appreciation for Patterson's assistance. Without Arthur's aid, the baseball public of Los Angeles might never have been made aware of O'Malley's true purpose in confining his American League neighbors to quarantine in Wrigley Field.

It is not for his own comfort that he denies a competitor space in his manger. It is for the good of the Angels and the good of the fans. No matter how great the personal sacrifice, he is resolved to protect Los Angeles and our national game from additional exposure to the squalor of the Coliseum. Now there is a man who stands on principle, whatever the cost to Autry and Reynolds.

This concern for the fans and the sport is a facet of Patterson's employer not previously revealed to the public. Yet not even there does his selfless regard for others cease.

"Fitting both the National and the American League schedules into the busy Coliseum program would have been an almost impossible task," Patterson discloses. "And other local sport promotions definitely would have suffered. As it is, several Dodger dates have had to be moved in order to handle the attractions of holiday priority over the ball club. In addition to baseball, the Coliseum also has commitments with U.S.C., U.C.L.A., the Rams, a spring football game, Mary's Hour, the Sheriff's Rodeo, the American Legion Fireworks show, the Shrine High School Football game and the Los Angeles "Times" Rams-Redskins pre-season football spectacular."

If, as Patterson says, these promotions have priority over the Dodgers, then they must have been already scheduled last December, when the Coliseum authorities announced that they could make dates available for virtually all the Angels' home games, if not for the entire schedule.

However, it may be that the people who run the Coliseum are just out for the rent and do not share O'Malley's solicitude for the Sheriff's Rodeo and the American Legion Fireworks show. Evidently there are no limits to the Good Neighbor's consideration for others.

With regard to the Cow Pasture's suitability for baseball, Patterson writes that "Smith was one of a galaxy of experts who freely predicted that all home run records would be broken in the Coliseum."

This is open to doubt, though perhaps Patterson's files are more complete than any available here, and memory can't always be trusted. As accurately as can be recalled, there never was any concern here about home run records, which are almost totally meaningless. No torchlight parades were organized when the Giants of 1947 set the major league record of 221 home runs, there was no dancing in the streets nine years later when the Reds tied the mark.

What has been pointed out here is that Cow Pasture is unfair to pitchers and also unfair to hitters. Little Leaguers can get home runs on pop flies over that screen in leftfield. Honest line drives good for four bases in any responsible park are cut to singles by the same screen.

The fact that a park may be unfair to good hitters does not render it less unfair to pitchers. It is simply unfair. The late John Lardner, who wasn't especially reverent about sports and studiously avoided overstatement, described it as an "immoral" ball park.

Still, it's flattering to be bracketed in a "galaxy of experts," even mistaken experts.

The Drooling-Delivery Problem

June 1961   New York

The rule is No. 6.02 and it declares: "The pitcher shall not be allowed to—(1) apply a foreign substance of any kind to the ball; (2) expectorate either on the ball or his glove; (3) rub the ball on his glove, person or clothing; (4) deface the ball in any manner; (5) deliver what is called the 'shine' ball, 'spit' ball, 'mud' ball, or 'emery' ball. The pitcher, of course, is allowed to rub the ball between his bare hands.

"Penalty—For violation of any part of this rule the umpire shall at once order the pitcher from the game, and in addition he shall be automatically suspended for a period of 10 days, on notice from the President of the League."

It seems clear enough, yet the chances are there is more misinformation current on this subject than on any other topic in sports.

The matter of the drooling delivery is in the news once more, and this time for a change the discussion does not concern Selva Lewis Burdette jr., the Milwaukee hero whose relative humidity has been a controversial issue for years and years. Recently the insanitary but elusive spitter won a powerful ally when Joe Cronin, president of the American League, no less, implied that he saw nothing sinful in saliva. Mike Higgins, manager of the Red Sox, concurs, and so does the baseball commissioner unofficially. For years Ford Frick has been saying, "Bring back the spitter," in informal conversations, but if he ever urged the rule makers to action nothing was done about it.

It was 1920 when the spit ball was declared verboten, with the proviso that big league pitchers already accustomed to slobbering on the sphere would not be required to break this untidy habit. Last of the licensed droolers was Burleigh Grimes, who ran dry with Bloomington in the Three-Eye League in 1935.

Myths can grow tall in four decades. Fans today who never saw a kosher spitter thrown will tell you that the damp delivery was banned because it is difficult to control and consequently a menace to life and limb, or because it is unsportsmanlike, or because it might offend fastidious customers, or because there is something intrinsically dishonest, not to say immoral, about moistening the hide of a dead horse.

In a baseball novel by an author born in 1922, a pitcher wiped his sweaty brow with his fingertips and threw a juicy curve. Though he had never employed this sordid tactic before, he controlled the pitch perfectly, breaking it over for a third strike. The catcher, the third baseman, the leftfielder, the batter and all his comrades on the bench and even people watching on television—everybody, in fact, except the umpire—instantly recognized the loathsome thing with grief and shock. The miscreant's father, an old sandlot left-hander himself, wept.

That was a few years ago. Today if a pitcher sneaked in a soggy one, his crime could go undetected except in the radio-television booth, where the eagles of electronics can identify curves, sliders, sinkers, screwballs, knucklers, fork balls and palm balls at 300 yards.

Well sir, the fact is that in 1920 the baseball people and the fans were power-happy. Babe Ruth had shattered all records by hitting 29 home runs in 1919 and would belt 54 in 1920. In spite of ugly rumors soon to be confirmed by the disclosure that the 1919 World Series had been crooked, customers were tearing their pants getting up gold to see the Babe swing.

Club owners of that time were not like today's sportsmen. They liked money. To encourage the long hitters and stimulate business they hopped up the ball and forbade doctoring the hide—packing the seams with mud, buffing up a shiny spot, roughening the cover with emery paper, lubricating it with spittle or using any other artificial aid to make a pitch misbehave.

That is the real and only reason why these useful devices are prohibited. The spitter never was more lethal than the fast ball, nor less godly. Thrown by a man who has mastered the delivery, it is not more difficult to control. Slobberers like Spittin' Bill Doak, Clarence Mitchell, Red Faber and Frank Shellenback weren't notorious for braining batters, and if Burleigh Grimes occasionally tucked one under a guy's chin or stuck it in his ear, this was due more to the venom in his soul than the slippery elm in his mouth.

With a two-day stubble on his jowls, eyes blazing with hate and yellow fangs bared, old Burleigh wasn't exactly a pretty sight as he drooled or pretended to drool into his cupped paws, but he was a sight to remember.

The spitter was not only a serviceable tool in the pitcher's trade, but apparently it was one he could use without great physical hardship. Craftsmen like Grimes, Doak, Mitchell and Faber enjoyed exceptionally long careers and seemed immune to arm ailments.

It is the exception today when a starting pitcher lasts nine innings. He needs every weapon he can command, yet everybody picks on him and they even have rules against playful forms of retaliation like parting a hitter's hair with a high hard one.

It's high time the poor slob got a break. These days he can't even depend on his catcher having a raised eyelet on his mitt and carving up the ball for him now and then. Sure as anything, some interfering ape of an umpire would ring in a new ball on the very next pitch.

How the Yankees Got Roger Maris

August 1961   New York

People are saying Ralph Houk has done a great job in his first season as manager of the Yankees, and people are right. Succeeding Casey Stengel had to be the meanest assignment in baseball, because a standard of excellence had been set which would, by comparison, make any merely creditable showing look like rank failure.

At no time during Houk's administration have the Yankees looked bad, and right now they appear ready to rush off and get lost as they seldom were able to do in Stengel's twelve years.

People are also saying that Houk ought to pay his way into the ballpark, that he was handed a ready-made team which any dolt should be able to bring home in first place. If the gallant Major overhears talk like that he needn't be offended, for it puts him in the best possible company. People said the same about John McGraw and Connie Mack and Miller Huggins and Joe McCarthy and Casey Stengel.

"Who did he ever lick?" is a question that was asked about Jack Dempsey and Joe Louis and Rocky Marciano, and probably about Stanley Ketchel and John L. Sullivan and John Broughton. The answer, of course, is that they licked the best of their time in their league, as

126

the Yankees did for Huggins and McCarthy and Stengel and are doing for Houk.

It is true, of course, that Houk has the horses, that he was given the horses. Not even Eddie Arcaro ever rode faster than his mount could run. It is also true that Houk has one big thing going for him that was only beginning to go for Stengel when he departed by request. He has Roger Maris as a full-fledged, established regular on his team.

Presenting Maris as the key to the Yankees' success may seem like suggesting that he is a more valuable ball player than Mickey Mantle or Elston Howard or Tony Kubek or Bill Skowron and Yogi Berra or Whitey Ford. No such comparisons are intended. All that is argued here is that Maris is a first-rate ball player who was exactly the man the Yankees had needed for a half dozen years.

He is the left-handed power hitter they hadn't had as a regular since Tommy Henrich, the one big guy they needed to collaborate with Berra in giving the attacks continuity and balance.

A good deal has been made of the fact that Houk has thrown away Stengel's book on the two-platoon system and, whenever the men were fit, played the same regular in the same position every day. Hardly anybody realizes that Casey would have been delighted to do the same, if his teams had enjoyed the balance which Maris has given to Houk's team.

It was back in 1957 when Maris was a rookie with the Indians that George Weiss' keen teutonic eye lighted on him. Maris was then 22 years old. He had never batted .300 in any league better than the Three-Eye. When he swung, though, he took a full riffle. He hit fourteen home runs for Cleveland that year.

"That's the young guy we've been looking for," Weiss said. "The left-handed hitter who could balance our attack." He couldn't get him, though. Frank Lane was the Indians' general manager then and he wouldn't deal with New York.

Chatting with Arnold Johnson, then owner of the Kansas City Athletics, Weiss remarked, "If you ever get a chance to make a deal with Cleveland insist on getting a young outfielder named Maris." The Indians were fairly well staffed then with outfielders named Rocky Colavita, Jim Busby, Al Smith, Sam Mele and Gene Woodling.

The following June the Indians and Athletics did make a deal. Kansas City gave Vic Power and Woodie Held for Dick Tomanek, Preston Ward and Roger Maris. Frank Lane extracted one promise, that if the Athletics did any business with the Yankees that year they would not let Maris go to New York. He couldn't bind them into eternity.

Maris was good in Kansas City that year and good for about half the next year, which was 1959. He was hurt for part of the latter season. In December the Athletics sent him to New York along with Kent Hadley and Joe DeMaestri, getting Don Larsen, Marv Throneberry, Hank Bauer and Norm Siebern. It seemed at the time that the Yankees were giving up plenty for a guy who had shown only flashes of class.

It shouldn't be necessary to mention who won the American League's Most Valuable Player prize last year, who led the league with 112 runs-batted-in.

The Yankees no longer have George Weiss, who got Maris for them, nor Casey Stengel, who put him in right-field, but they've got Maris.

After the Blood, Sweat and Cheers Are Over

August 1961   New York

When the blood, sweat and cheers of the current baseball season have been strained through a comptometer
and reduced to columns of figures in agate type, the
thoughtful historian will have this to say about 1961:

It was the year when two muscular pretenders to the
mantle of Babe Ruth lifted the mortgage on Joe
Cronin's old homestead in much the same manner as the
Babe himself saved the game from possible ruin forty
summers earlier.

It was a year which demonstrated in striking fashion
how far the National League had surpassed the American
in achieving an even distribution of strength.

It was the year when Charles O. Finley, out of the
wisdom gleaned from five months' experience in the game,
successfully challenged Calvin Griffith for distinction as
the Club Owner Most Likely to Louse Up Any Franchise
He Gets His Cotton-Pickin' Paws On.

It was the year Philip K. Wrigley proved conclusively
that eight heads were better than one, provided the one
was worn by a guy with guts enough to manage the
Phillies.

There can never be an accurate measure of Mickey
Mantle's and Roger Maris' contribution to the finan-

cial well-being of the American League, because there is no way of knowing how far business would have declined if neither were threatening Babe Ruth's home run record.

However, the only team in the league that has prevented the Yankees from making a travesty of the pennant race is Detroit, and it is not easy to take the Tigers seriously. They're stubborn little rascals, though; if they can keep the leaders in their sights the rest of this month they'll do a thriving trade in New York, Sept. 1, 2, and 3, and during the Yankees' last Detroit visit in mid-September.

In eight other cities, all pretense of championship competition was abandoned long ago. From Boston to Los Angeles, the ball parks would be left to the bats and owls if it weren't for the excitement generated by Company M's pursuit of Babe Ruth's ghost.

As it is, teams with little or no appeal for metropolitan fans hit the jackpot when they visit Yankee Stadium, and rake in the swag at home when Mantle and Maris come calling. By maintaining baseball interest everywhere at a level far above normal for a season like this, the Smashers help keep the turnstiles spinning even when they're not in the neighborhood.

No player since Ruth himself ever had more persuasive arguments than these two can offer at contract time next winter. Every owner in the league owes them money.

Except for the ghastly Phillies, every team in the National League is closer to the pace than its opposite number in the American. Even the hydra-headed Cubs, twenty-three games behind Cincinnati yesterday, were not so far back as Kansas City, Washington, Minnesota, Los Angeles or Boston.

In three years three different teams—Milwaukee, Los Angeles and Pittsburgh—have won the National League pennant, and Cincinnati may make it four for four. In addition, the end of the 1959 season found two teams in first place; the Dodgers had to survive a play-off with the Braves.

The American League pennant has flown in the Bronx for five of the last six years and ten of the last twelve. If it is conceded that the Yankee brass does a better job year after year than anybody else in baseball, it follows that practically everybody in the National does better than the Yankees' opposition.

In the National League they set up champions only to knock them down. In the American the standard procedure, outside New York, is to sit on a rock and cry.

In this department, nobody has displayed more natural talent than Charles O. Finley, who set up shop in Kansas City in April and is already bleating that "there are places where we might be wanted." Off his performance to date, he may be overrating the hospitality of other cities.

Finley must be the quickest study ever cast in the role of baseball expert. After fifty-five years in the game, Connie Mack freely acknowledged that he hadn't found all the answers. After less than three months, Finley knew more than his manager, Joe Gordon, whom he fired summarily. Now it is reported that Frank Lane, the general manager with the strongest stomach in baseball, is fed up.

Charges of meddling have brought no denial. "As an owner," Finley says, "I wouldn't make a $5,000,000 investment without having brains enough to take part in it. I have to take full responsibility for success or failure of this team."

He is bitter about newspaper criticism and aggrieved to find his welcome wearing thin in the prairie metropolis. In the latter respect, he may have just cause for complaint, for he has, after all, brought a rare distinction to Kansas City. For the city of his adoption he has produced something no other city in the major leagues ever could boast—a tenth-place club.

This is Sport . . .

September 1961   New York

With breakfast came the news from Monza in Italy. One paragraph reported: "The race went on. For the next two hours cars roared around the track past the bodies of the dead, strewn over the grass and covered with newspapers."

This is sport. This was the Grand Prix of Italy, where an automobile driver named Wolfgang von Trips spun through the infield crowd and killed himself, taking 11 customers with him. Twenty-six others were maimed.

It wasn't Monza's biggest slaughter. The record score there for one car is 28. In 1958 at Le Mans in France, a Mercedes bagged 53.

If auto racing doesn't send you, you're a square. It is recognized by those in the know as the purest of art forms, the noblest of sports, the heroic way of life. One thing the greaseniks share in common is the gift of explaining away needless killing. They do so in angry letters, generally attributing it all to "newspaper sensationalism" or "yellow journalism," often abusing the dead, for getting killed, with shocking vituperation.

"Casualties do occur," they concede, "but you must not blame the sport for this." Hereafter, then, let us blame badminton for it, at least until we meet a senile auto racer.

Saturday was better. Saturday was wonderful. First there was 21-inch baseball from the Stadium with the Yankees getting a thin lead on the Indians after four innings. No early home runs for Mantle or Maris, though. When each had gone to the plate twice, a flick of the dial tuned in ABC's "Wide World of Sports" and a remarkable show called "Inside Football."

In an exhibition between the San Diego Chargers and Dallas Texans of the American Football League, they had the quarterbacks wired for sound, had cameras and cables on the sidelines to trip runners on sweeps, had a boom camera high over the field, and even permitted a cameraman to lug his gear into the huddle.

Such shenanigans in a championship game would have turned a football buff pale with horror but in the circumstances it was fascinating. In the huddle the viewer could hear the quarterback: "All right now, heads up for an audible. Full right, 55 trap, on two."

Up in the pressbox, George Ratterman eavesdropped on the huddle and translated the signals aloud to Jim McKay. Naturally, the defensive team's coaches would arrange to do the same in a real game.

Now it was time to catch the fillies in the Matron Stakes, but with a hurried stop first in the Stadium, where Willie Kirkland whacked one into the seats to bring Cleveland level in the score. While Wynn Elliott was interviewing Patrice Jacobs before the Matron, the first half ended in San Diego and viewers on Channel 7 were transported to Ruidoso Downs, N.M., for a quarter-horse race worth $202,000.

This was a dandy bit. There were views of the grounds, where even the kids wore 10-gallon hats, and a brief but interesting illustrated lecture on the differences in conformation between the thoroughbred and the quarter-horse. Then the ponies raced 440 yards down a straight-away—unfortunately obscured by the grandstand's shadow as they came toward the finish—with the microphone picking up cowboy whoops as the unbeaten favorite, Bunny's Barmaid, ran second.

Back, quickly, to Belmont. When Willie Shoemaker brought Cicada around the leaders, she drew clear in the stretch. At the 70-yard pole it was all hers, so click went the dial and here was Maris hitting No. 56. The Yankees were now three runs behind, however.

It was still half-time in San Diego. There were cameras and mikes in the dressing room where Texans, trailing by four touchdowns, talked about what was going wrong. Not much of this was audible.

The magic carpet returned to Yankee Stadium. The Yankees put on a four-run rush in the ninth to win, 8-7. Not a moment too soon, either, for the tennis players were already in the semi-finals of the National Singles Championships at Forest Hills.

Australia's Rod Laver and England's Mike Sangster were picked up with the score 10-all in games for the first set. In spite of Sangster's really big service, Laver won in a lively match, employing his great advantage in international experience. Video tape made it possible to catch a little of a match already completed between Don Emerson and Rafael Osuna.

Richard Harding Davis should have done his traveling on the same expense account.

Babe Ruth's Ghost

The Yankees won it early, and it didn't matter, some-how. Everybody knew they were going to win the pen-nant. What everybody wanted to know was, how about Roger Maris and the great ghost-hunt?

"If Maris has any class," a guy said, joking, after Maris went hitless in the first game of Tuesday's twi-night doubleheader, "he'll go empty tonight and then rap three tomorrow."

At this point Maris had 58 home runs. He did go empty in Tuesday's second game, so that he went to work last night needing two home runs to tie Babe Ruth's record 60, three to break it within the 154-game limit imposed by Ford Frick, the tradition-loving base-ball commissioner.

"I'll tell you how he'll do it," a romantic said before the game began. "First time up, he'll hit one. Next time he'll strike out. They'll walk him on his third trip but he'll smack No. 60 on his fourth. This'll be one of those games where he comes up five times. So on the last shot, he'll make it 61—and win the pennant in the bar-gain."

In Hollywood they would have done it that way, but this is Baltimore—Babe Ruth's home town. Maris got No. 59 and he's the first since Ruth or before him to reach that figure. But the Yankees could have and would have won without his hit.

It's hard to describe how this was, the last crazy rush in pursuit of Babe Ruth's ghost. Maris himself had been saying right along that he took no stock in the commis-sioner's view that Ruth's record couldn't be broken un-less it was done in a season of 154 games, such as Ruth used to play. Nobody doubts that the fellow will hit 61 or more before the expanded season of 162 games ends. Just the same, Maris was keenly aware of the deadline. So were the 21,032 witnesses who saw him come up against Milt Pappas in the first inning. Pappas is big and tough and able, but at least he's right-handed and he pitches like people.

That is, he pitches fast balls and curves. He must have looked good to Maris, a left-handed hitter. In the first game Tuesday evening, Maris had to swing against Steve Barber, the youngest and meanest left-handed pitcher in the American League.

In Tuesday's second game they hit him in the face with two knuckle-ball throwers, and hardly anybody hits the knuckler far.

Last night the wind that had been blowing in from right field moderated, but on his first time up Maris got only a piece of the ball and pulled a line drive to Earl Robinson in right.

The crowd relaxed for a while, making no great disturbance when Bill Skowron's triple and Cletis Boyer's single put the Yankees in front, 1-0, in the second inning.

It was still 1-0 and Pappas was still pitching when Maris came up in the third inning with one out and nobody on base. In fact, the Yankees' Ralph Terry was pitching a perfect game up to this point, and he was destined to wind up with a four-hitter.

Maris took the first pitch for a ball. He swung at the second and missed. The third was low for a second ball.

The fourth—well, there never was a moment's question about the fourth. Maris nailed it with that lovely, level swing of his and it looked so remarkably easy. Even as it left the bat, customers in the sparsely settled seats in right were on their feet getting ready to scrap for it.

Yogi Berra followed with a home run and the Yankees scored again before the inning ended, on a single by John Blanchard and a double by Elston Howard.

Nobody cared much, though. Everybody knew the Yankees were going to win the pennant: it was only the ghost-hunt that counted.

By the time Maris came up again, a tall kid named Dick Hall was pitching. Hall is a sterling young man out of nearby Towson, Md., whom Branch Rickey snagged off the Swarthmore campus a few years back when Ricky was running a day nursery in Pittsburgh.

Hall knocked around a few years before anybody discovered what he was good at. He is good at throwing strikes, on the very edge of the plate.

Hall fired one over the outside corner and Maris took the strike. Hall brushed the inside edge, and Maris took his second strike. He swung at the third, which was also inside, and pulled a screaming foul to right. He just plain missed the next.

There was one out again when Maris came up in the seventh. The first time they had faced each other, Hall had thrown nothing but strikes. This was the second time, and again they were all strikes. Maris took one, fouled one and flied out to right on the third.

Roger was the Yankees' last hitter, with two out and none on in the ninth. Now Hoyt Wilhelm was throwing that nauseous knuckler. Maris took a half-swing on the first pitch and fouled it back. He took a half-swing at the second and dribbled down the first-base line where Wilhelm fielded the ball and tagged him out. The crowd had been giving off animal noises, but suddenly there was an odd silence. The great chase was ended.

There is, however, one bit of good news. Seems there's a new strip-tease artist playing the joints, a smasher, they say. Her name is Mickey Maris.

Sam Snead Runs Afoul P.G.A. Panjandrums

October 1961   New York

Some of the finest golfers in the world are hacking through the gorse and bracken and thistle and furze of Lytham-St. Anne's beside the Irish Sea this week end in the Ryder Cup matches, a competition that has been dishonored by the pipsqueak panjandrums of the Professional Golfers' Association of America.

By tossing Sam Snead off the American team on a trumped-up technicality, the P.G.A. leaders have done shocking injustice to the most celebrated player in the game, short-changed the Ryder Cup galleries, embarrassed both the United States and British players, performed a disservice to the organization they represent and put themselves away as vindictive tinpot tyrants unworthy of the jobs they hold.

It was almost painful to encounter Snead in New York during the World Series and discover how deeply hurt he was. Throughout his professional life he has conscientiously heeded Mr. Khayyam's advice to take the cash and let the credit go, but his cut went deeper than the wallet.

At 49, Sam would have been the oldest man ever to compete in this biennial skirmish. Starting in 1937—the same year that Dai Rees, Great Britain's 1961 captain, first made the team—he failed only once to qualify for the American team and only once was he beaten in the singles. The players who recaptured the Cup with him in 1959 gave him the well-deserved honor of the captaincy.

Snead's troubles began when, instead of traveling 2,-000 miles at his own expense to play in the Portland, Ore., Open, he accepted an invitation to a one-day pro-amateur affair in Cincinnati, comparatively close to home. It was more an exhibition than a tournament and it was only at the suggestion of somebody in Cincinnati that Sam made belated application to the Portland tournament committee for permission to play the pro-am.

He was aware of the P.G.A. by-law, never approved by the membership, prohibiting top money-winners and holders of certain designated championships from participating in any tournaments, excluding exhibitions, whose dates conflict with the P.G.A.-approved events. However, he was confident the rule did not apply to him because the P.G.A., forbidding Arnold Palmer, Gary Player and Stan Leonard to compete for the Canada Cup last spring because of a conflict in dates, did allow Sam to play.

According to reputable and angry members of the P.G.A., the Portland people were disposed to give Snead the permission he sought, and refused only at the insistence of the P.G.A. leadership. Anyhow, Sam was already playing in Cincinnati when a telegram denying permission arrived. He withdrew promptly.

It was clear that the P.G.A. gestapo was reversing itself. Snead won the Tournament of Champions before the Canada Cup; he has won nothing since. If the no-conflict rule didn't apply to him at Canada Cup time, it does not apply now. Yet for appearing in Cincinnati he was fined $500 and suspended for six months. If this wasn't a face-saving job by the officials, then it had all the earmarks of personal persecution.

As though inviting the public to decide which it was, the P.G.A. shop stewards made the injustice retroactive by flinging Snead off the Ryder Cup team. Cup players are chosen on the basis of points won in tournament play through the year. Sam had qualified well before he sinned in Cincinnati. Indeed, he had worked hard to qualify, entering tournaments he would have passed up if he hadn't needed the points.

Doug Ford, 11th in the point standings, was invited to take Sam's place on the 10-man squad. He protested, accepting reluctantly only when it became clear that the bureaucrats would go clear to the bottom of the list for a substitute, if necessary. It is understood that the uniform already tailored for Snead had to be shortened only about half-an-inch for Doug.

Ford is a fine golfer and worthy representative of his country. He didn't qualify, however, and he is uncomfortably, unhappily, aware of it.

The P.G.A. bosses have abridged America's right to be represented by her 10 best players, as established in competition. They have denied the British players their right to try for a clear-cut victory against an opponent at full strength. They have deprived British fans of the pleasure of following the player who invariably attracts greater galleries than any other.

The only reason for putting pressure on the top players to appear in approved tournaments is to protect the sponsors who put up their money. The sponsors must now get along for six months without the biggest drawing card in the game.

Jimmy Demaret, invited to comment on the sorry business, groped for an adjective and came up with "asinine." Jimmy is a notoriously nice guy, though. Speaks kindly of everybody.

Notre Dame-Syracuse Rhubarb . . . The Rulebook

November 1961   New York

The burning question today is: Just how high can higher education get? A little learning, Mr. Pope observed, is a dangerous thing. On the basis of their attainments in the esoteric field of football rules, Asa Bushnell, Commissioner of the Eastern College Athletic Conference; Bill Reed, of the Big Ten; gentle General Bob Neyland, chairman of the Rules Committee, and innumerable lesser authorities have declared that the officials erred in permitting Notre Dame to beat Syracuse, 17-15, last Saturday. The gentlemen are mistaken.

Now, five days after the event, comes a higher power to save the old homestead for Notre Dame. From some monastic cell on the campus outside South Bend, somebody has flushed a scholar so steeped in basic Chinese that he has been able to read the rule book, actually translate it, and point to a paragraph which clearly, unmistakably supports the officials and entitles Notre Dame to victory.

The paragraph was written by the late E. C. Krieger, of Columbus, Ohio, a veteran Big Ten official who compiled for the 1961 Rule Book the "Questions and Answers" section subtitled, "Official Interpretations of Certain Moot Points in the Football Rules." The first paragraph under "Definitions," concerning "possession with reference to a kicked ball," reads as follows:

Although a free ball, a scrimmage kick from behind Team A's (Notre Dame's) line is treated as though in possession of Team A if the penalty for roughing the kicker is accepted.

Out of an ignorant but touching confidence in the Messrs. Bushnell, Reed, Neyland et al., it had been the purpose here to exhort the football brass at Notre Dame to make a thorough examination of conscience, arrive at a firm purpose of amendment, and renounce, disgorge and yield up a victory not earned under the rules.

The splendid moral point would have been made that when the cashier gives you $10 change for a $1 bill, the only decent thing to do is give it back.

It would have been explained that no blame attached to the Notre Dame team, which was in no way responsible for the foul that started the rhubarb, the official ruling which dealt with it, the injustice to Syracuse which resulted or the commotion that followed.

The fault, it was going to be said, lay with the stupidity of the rule makers, the indescribably muddy prose which conceals the meaning of the code, and knot-headed officials who couldn't understand it.

Now it develops that there was no error on the field, no injustice to Syracuse. On the contrary, it was Notre Dame who was fouled by Syracuse, but it was Syracuse who hollered copper.

The rule involved, or specifically, a sneaky little gimmick in the rule, remains an indefensible bit of idiocy that cries aloud for editing.

Because the man kicking a football and the man holding the ball for a place kick are unable to protect themselves against a rushing defense, the rule book properly gives them protection. We've all seen penalties assessed scores of times for roughing the kicker. Almost invariably the foul occurs when the ball is in the air; the play is called back and the offending team penalized 15 yards. (It happened yesterday when the Packers played the Lions.)

However, it is further provided that if this foul occurs as time expires, then the game ends and it is not a foul unless the ball was in the offended team's possession. In other words, although roughing the kicker is forbidden at all other times, on the last play of the game the defense may use zip-guns, machetes and brass knuckles with impunity. Somebody might get flung into jail, but there will be no 15-yard penalty.

The authorities who declared the officials in error did so under the misapprehension that a kicked ball is not in the kicking team's possession. The late Mr. Krieger makes it clear that it is.

Films of the game show that as Notre Dame's Joe Perkowski attempted a 54-yard field goal in the dying seconds, he was hit by a Syracuse end named Walt Sweeney and parlayed into George Sefcik, who had teed up the ball. The head linesman deemed this a foul, reported it as such to the referee, and although time had run out, Perkowski was given a second chance from shorter range. He made it this time and Notre Dame, beaten by 15-14 when time ran out, got three points to win.

Until the faulty technicality regarding "possession" was raised a day or so later, everybody concerned was satisfied with Miss Gertrude Stein's dictum that a foul is a foul is a foul is a foul, on the first play of the game or the last.

Now hear this: The late Mr. Krieger had a nickname. His friends called him "Irish." A coincidence.

Year of the Proletariat

December 1961   New York

Snowdrifts in New York and the high-jump bar in Madison Square Garden both reached record heights as the sports year of 1961 began. It was to be the Year of the Proletariat—the year of a Marxist in half-column britches named Valery Brumel—the year of Carry Back, the Great Commoner—the year of Roger Maris, a baseball player with a plebeian batting average of .270.

While Russia's Brumel was out-jumping America's John Thomas in the indoor track meets, Carry Back was out-running all the three-year-olds in Florida sunshine. Ball players were just starting to work up a sweat when Floyd Patterson, heavyweight cahmpion of the world,

141

smote Ingemar Johansson on the ear and Ingemar swooned. He awoke to find himself gazing into the beady eye of a man from the Internal Revenue Service.

"Call it an even million, chum," the tax collector said. "No? Oh, well, I'll take the purse."

In training camp, Maris was only one member of an all-star cast that would, everybody was sure, brighten Ralph Houk's first year as manager of the Yankees. The Yankees couldn't beat anybody in the exhibition games, though. Neither could the Cincinnati Reds. To the experts assembled in St. Petersburg, this proved that spring training scores were meaningless; to those in Tampa, it showed the weakness of the Reds.

Then all of a sudden the baseball season was open, with ten teams jockeying for position in the American League, eight in the National, and one owner in Kansas City giving new meaning to the ballplayer's adjective, "bush."

In May the trail led to Louisville, where Carry Back won the Kentucky Derby, to Baltimore, where Carry Back won the Preakness and to Belmont, where Carry Back went lame and didn't win the Belmont Stakes and racing's Triple Crown. The Yankees and Reds took command in the big leagues and Ford Frick, the baseball commissioner, ruled that if any hitter was going to break Babe Ruth's record of 60 home runs, he'd have to do it inside 154 games.

The owner in Kansas City fired his manager.

Both Maris and Mickey Mantle were hot in pursuit of Ruth's record. Hotter still were the wrangles regarding Ford Frick's asterisks. It made no difference, dissenters insisted, that expansion to a 10-team league had added eight games to the Yankees' schedule and thus created additional opportunities to hit home runs. A season was a season for a' that.

Kelso, the greatest gelding since Exterminator, took all the weight they piled onto him and won the handicap Triple Crown—the Metropolitan, the Suburban and the Brooklyn. The horses moved to Saratoga and the two-year-olds looked fine.

Archie Moore, boy patriarch, dropped the boom on
142

an in-offensive Italian named Giulio Rinaldi. "Burny, burny, mustn't touch!" a process-server cried as Archie reached for his $81,000 purse. Christmas would find him still reaching.

Both the Yankees and Reds looked like shoo-ins, yet crowds packed the ball parks to see the gaunt blond swing for the fences. He professed to be unconcerned about Frick's asterisk, yet by the time the Yankees played Baltimore, Sept. 20, in their 154th game, Maris was literally losing his hair. He got his 59th home run that night, and Ruth's record stood, even though Roger was to finish the long season with 61.

In the first World Series game, the Yankees' Whitey Ford shut out the Reds, 2-0. It was Ford's third straight World Series shutout, threatening the record of 29⅔ consecutive scoreless innings which Ruth set as a pitcher in 1916 and 1918. The Reds won the second game and the teams went to Cincinnati all square.

"Yes," said Jim Brosnan, the Reds' relief pitcher, when visitors remarked on the snug dimensions of Crosley Field, "a pitcher can't afford to make mistakes here. In fact, it's a small town. You can't afford any mistakes."

With the score tied in the ninth inning of the third game, Bob Purkey made a mistake pitching to Maris. The ball hasn't been seen since. The Reds disappeared two days later, shortly after Ford rubbed out Ruth's record.

Coaches Know Who's Boss

January 1962   New York

In column seven, a member of the Board of Supervisors at Louisiana State was saying: "It's time these coaches realize they have moral obligations as well as character-building obligations. Most of them regard contracts as just another piece of paper. It's time somebody takes a stand against them."

In column five a dispatch from Lexington, Ky., reported: "Blanton Collier, who faced the almost impossible task of replacing Paul (Bear) Bryant, was fired yesterday as head football coach at the University of Kentucky. The University's Athletic Board voted to buy the remaining three years of Collier's contract."

Back in column seven, another of the L.S.U. supervisors was stating his conviction that Paul Dietzel would resist the passes Army has been making at him and work out the four years remaining in his contract in Baton Rouge.

"I don't believe Paul will break his contract," this one said. "I don't believe Paul will be happy in joining the fiddle-footed coaches who walk off the job and have no respect for the sanctity of a contract. If the question comes before the Board, I will not vote to release him."

In Kentucky, Collier, 55, said he had no immediate plans. "Football has been my life," he said.

It isn't often that Mr. N. Webster can be accused of goofing off, but here is one instance where he falls down on the job. Sanctity, he explains in his popular book, is a noun meaning: "1. State or quality of being sacred or holy; holiness of life and character; saintliness; godliness. 2. Sacredness; solemnity; inviolability; religious binding force; as, the sanctity of an oath."

He fails to add the obvious example: "As, the sanctity of a contract with a coach whose teams win football games." This is important because saintliness and godliness are coachly attributes only when the teams gets invited to the Orange Bowl. There is no sanctity of contract with the coach whose team loses half its games.

Fiddle-bottomed educators recognize no moral obligations when the team gets licked. When it comes to respecting contracts, these preceptors of youth and custodians of character are a fair match for the lower forms of labor boss. Shamelessly, they make the shameful pretense that by greasing the skids with money they are keeping their end of the bargain.

What they are doing, of course, is barely meeting the legal obligations which they cannot evade. They contracted to employ the coach for an agreed period, and when they buy out of that promise they put themselves away as welshers, to say nothing of the mortal injury such summary dismissal does to the coach's professional standing and earning potential.

Regarding a contract as "just another piece of paper" is deplorable, but the coach who does so is only recognizing a fact of life. He knows from the bitter experience of his clan that even if the college authorities are unwilling to weasel out of their bargain, there are innumerable ways of making his position insupportable and his life unendurable.

The "Goodbye Harry Club" in Stuhldreher's day at Wisconsin was a disgraceful example of the pressures that can be brought to bear by undergraduates, alumni or townsfolk.

When the late Herman Hickman had winning teams at Yale and was doubling as a television entertainer, poet and after-dinner speaker, Yalies went around cooing that he was not only a great coach but also the most scintillating wit and gifted artist of his time. He could stir them to frenzied cheering by touching a match to a cigar.

When the supply of gristle ran short, you could hear them around the Yale Club saying, "It wouldn't be like this if we had a football coach instead of a fat hillbilly comic." A reformed rassler, Herman was no stranger to abuse from crowds, but the snipers' fire got so heavy he resigned.

In the light of history, it is nauseating to hear educators prate of moral obligations and the sanctity of contracts. It is sickening to read a statement that says in effect:

"I am confident that our noble, and successful, coach would never dream of quitting us for a better job, and if the dirty hound does we'll show him who's boss around here."

The coach already knows who's boss. He found out when his predecessor was callously pitched into the street.

The Masters of Space

January 1962   New York

Some years ago, the tenant in this literary flophouse had the happy experience of learning at first hand how a treed raccoon feels when the hunt has closed in and the hounds are circling, snapping, leaping and yelping just below. It was during a World Series, not long after some admiring comments had appeared here regarding the ring-tailed wonders of radio and television who can perch on a cloud far above a ball park and confidently advise the listener that the shapeless blur he has just seen on his screen was a knee-high slider that just tickled the outside corner.

Far from appreciating this tribute, the masters of space were furious. They closed in at the bar in press headquarters, yapping that they could too tell a screwball from a knuckler at long range, even though the pitch might completely deceive the professional at bat and it might be all the umpire could do to decide whether it was a strike or a ball.

It was fun facing that angry semi-circle and trying to placate them with a soft response: "What are you so sore about, fellows? I only called you a bunch of pretentious fakers."

Well, things have reached a pretty pass when this space is devoted to a defense of the space cadets of sports. Yet a magazine piece has come to attention which abuses the sportscasting clan so unfairly, with such unsightly disregard for truth, as to make martyrs of the victims and strip the criticism of validity.

The piece appears in a magazine of the performing arts called Show. It is entitled, "The Big Mouths," and carries the byline of Bill Davidson, a reformed hurdler from New York University who served a hitch as ghost-writer for the great fictioneer of radio, Bill Stern. Naturally, the author pads out the indictment by blowing the whistle

146

on his former boss but even there, where he ought to be on firm ground, he disqualifies himself.

"One day," he writes in an effort to illustrate Stern's renowned indifference to facts, "I decided to see just how far Stern would go. I made up the wildest cock-and-bull story my imagination could conceive. It was about a college track athlete who went to Finland to fight the Russians and defeated a whole battalion by throwing javelins with hand grenades tied to them.

"Then he was captured and escaped from the prison camp by pole-vaulting over the barbed-wire fence. He outran his pursuers (who were on skis) and just made it across the border into Sweden—after which he decided to become a priest. He taught philosophy and was track coach at an American Catholic college and rose to be a Cardinal in the Church.

"As I told this monumental series of lies, Stern became ecstatic, and I'm sure he would have used the concoction on the air. But when we came to the point where Stern ended most of his stories with the declamation: 'And that man is . . .' the only name I could think of was that of Alfred Paca, who also did coolie labor for Stern. So that was the end of that."

Lord knows, there was ground for complaint when Stern was abusing the credulity of adolescent sports buffs across the land, but this chump thinks the way to do the job is to put himself away as a fraud whose brazen fabrications were too strong for even Stern's stomach.

In this book, there are precious few sportscasters with professional standards higher than those of a fourth-rate vaudeville ham on the old Pantages circuit, but when this self-confessed humbug singles out individuals for attack, he unerringly impugns them for faults that aren't theirs.

Thus he declares that after Walter O'Malley decided to move the Dodgers to Los Angeles, Vince Scully, the Brooklyn broadcaster, "went through an entire half-season in Ebbets Field without once mentioning to his public that the team would not be there the following spring." The fact is that Scully went through entire seasons without mentioning this, because O'Malley kept his plans to himself—and even denied repeatedly that he had a plan —until after the World Series.

Don Dunphy, the most honest and accurate fight reporter on the air, is accused of talking "about the power-laden left hook of an overmatched middleweight who does nothing but paw feebly with that appendage for 10 rounds."

Yes, the prose is as rancid as that throughout.

Out of 2,000 words or so, it isn't easy to pick out the most outrageous misstatement, half-truth or unvarnished lie, but a personal favorite is this:

"The entire sports field has long been noted for its payola. Back in my Bill Stern days, I used to sit in the waiting room of Mike Jacobs' old Twentieth Century Sporting Club and see some of the most respected sportswriters in town walk in and openly receive their weekly pay envelopes from the cashier's window."

This has got to be a bald lie because sportswriters on the take aren't respected by anybody.

"I resigned my apprentice membership in the Sports Broadcasters' Association," the author concludes, implying that his ethical standards were the reason. This may have been a step in the right direction, but then he turned to writing.

New Guy at West Point ... Paul Dietzel

January 1962   New York

The philosophy that has served Paul Dietzel, Army's new football coach, since his beginning as an instructor in skull-cracking, was enunciated before he was born by Mr. Kipling:

> When 'Omer smote 'is bloomin' lyre,
>   He'd 'eard men sing by land an' sea;
> An' what he thought 'e might require,
>   'E went an' took—the same as me!

Dietzel's Homer is a composite, part Red Blaik, part Sid Gillman, part Bear Bryant, part Dave Nelson. Each had something Dietzel required and he went and took it, with full permission of the copyright owner. Naturally, he tossed his own assets into the pot, but being as honest as he is able, he has always been the first to acknowledge his debts to others.

As coach of Louisiana State's three-decker terror, Dietzel has been a demigod in the Deep South. Now, as drillmaster of the West Point forces, he becomes a figure commanding attention. Chances are fans in every section are curious about this young man, his personality, his professional qualifications, his approach to the job.

Well, he is a tall, attractive blond out of Ohio, poised and articulate. He played football at Miami of Ohio. He served as an assistant coach there, later worked under Gillman at Cincinnati and Bryant at Kentucky, and did two hitches on Blaik's staff at West Point.

Chances are not even he could tell exactly what each of these men taught him, but he was an alert and eager student and he has never grown too proud to learn from others. Gillman is something of an explorer, inventive and adventuresome. Bryant is tireless and dedicated. Blaik was the supreme drillmaster, a fundamentalist, and a stickler for infinite detail. (At West Point, the head coach dictated even such decisions as how to slice the oranges which the players would suck on the bench—into halves, quarters, or eighths.)

"One fall Col. Blaik was sick when he played Yale, a tough opponent that year," Dietzel says, recalling a lesson in sound football. "He was on the sideline but I was in charge of the team. We got a couple of quick touchdowns and were eating up yardage when a fourth-and-one situation came up just before the half ended.

" 'Kick it,' Col. Blaik said, but the kids wanted to go for first down and so did I. There was a time-out then, which gave me a chance to argue. I pointed out that the way our ground game was going we were a cinch to make first down and that would give us a chance for the third touchdown before the half ended.

" 'It's not good football,' Col. Blaik said, 'kick it.'

"So we punted to their five-yard line where they fumbled and we recovered and got the touchdown. Walking to the dressing room I said, 'Thank you, Coach, for Lesson No. 23,156.' "

When Dietzel went to Baton Rouge, he felt that L.S.U. lacked the depth and versatility of its top opponents. He decided he could compete on even terms only if he could utilize every talent available. Both Gillman at Cincinnati and Blaik at West Point had been communicants of the two-platoon faith, training boys as defensive or offensive specialists to polish their natural skills.

After evolving a system of testing and grading the players, he picked the eleven best all-around athletes for his first team. From the remainder, he chose the eleven likeliest candidates for offense, whose abilities might be limited to running, blocking or passing. This was the second team. From the rest he chose the most aggressive for a third team. This unit might be slower than the others and far less nifty, but zealots could be taught the head-butting fundamentals of defense.

For morale purposes Dietzel rejected the standard designations of first, second and third teams. He called the two-way group his "White" team, the offensive unit the "Go" team and for the left-overs he borrowed the name "Chinese Bandits," which somebody at Cincinnati had coined in similar circumstances during his term there.

The players practiced in units, played as units, unconsciously fell into the habit of eating, dressing and socializing as units, and to the coach's gratification a special esprit de corps came to characterize each group. Devoting most of their practice time to defensive work—while the "Go" team concentrated on offense and the "Whites" divided their time equally—the Chinese Bandits became more ardent pursuers and harder tacklers than their more gifted schoolmates.

They also became one of the most celebrated undergraduate groups in the country, due to the colorful name and its connotations of bloodthirsty savagery. They had their own rooting section, togged out in coolie hats. Instead of fighting to advance from the third team, kids begged to be assigned to the Bandits.

It was a tremendous con job that worked. Having borrowed this idea, Dietzel went to Dave Nelson, the ingenious little guy at Delaware who had developed refinements on the split-T formation with novel line-spacings, cross-blocking assignments and that sort of thing. Forrest Evashevski at Iowa was killing 'em in the Big Ten with Nelson's stuff, and once he got it working Dietzel killed 'em with it in the South.

The point is, Paul Dietzel never took credit for what he borrowed. He not only told everybody where he got it, but he put it in writing. Army's new guy–is that sort of guy. Meanwhile, a fellow remarked to Dave Nelson that football coaches were no smarter than baseball writers; just as the latter always choose a pennant-winner as Manager of the Year, the coaches always pick a guy with an undefeated team as Coach of the Year. The unbeaten team may use Nelson's stuff, but there's never one vote for the inventor as Coach of the Year.

"That's where you're wrong," Dave Nelson's aid cheerfully said. "There's a vote for Nelson every year. One vote."

N.C.A.A. Wowsers vs. A.A.U. Waxworks

January 1962   New York

Men who devote their lives to children's games are so infantile in their approach to the world that to take sides in their spats is like offering to punch a neighbor in the nose because his brat has beat up our little Orvie. That is the feeling here about the current hair-pull between the Amateur Athletic Union and the *mens sana* mob, as represented by the National Collegiate Athletic Association, the National College Track Coaches' Association, the National Association of Gymnastic Coaches and other such intellectuals.

For about a year, guerrilla groups on the campuses have been fomenting a revolt against the A.A.U. with a view toward taking over administration of amateur sports. Nobody has paid much attention because nobody, outside the few men who have made a living working for the A.A.U., gives a whoop whether the organization survives or perishes.

Reluctant though a guy may be to wound the feelings of the immature, it has to be said that nobody ever went to a track meet to see Avery Brundage or Dan Ferris or Pinky Sober strut across the infield with his boiled shirt bulging out to here. As long as the runners run and the jumpers jump and the gymnasts compete, the public won't care who runs the show.

If the wowsers of the N.C.A.A. think they can do a better job than the waxworks effigies of the A.A.U., then let them try. But we ought to remember that the campus intelligentsia have never yet been able to write a football rule book which they themselves can read and understand.

These are the guys who want to take over other sports, when they haven't begun to master their own. Chaos will replace confusion, anarchy will substitute for inefficiency. Their very tactics in organizing the revolt, by circulating a loaded questionnaire which betrays their ignorance of the problems, has brought shocked protests from the solid college coaches like Bob Giegengack, George Eastment and Brutus Hamilton.

No doubt there have been many occasions when the guys who ran the A.A.U. were wrong-headed, stubborn, ill-advised or uninformed. Unquestionably they have made a lot of mistakes. But who is going to do better? Walter Byers and his crowd, for heaven's sake?

The N.C.A.A. has no jurisdiction off the campuses. There are a great many top-drawer athletes who have no college affiliation. They are card-carrying members of the A.A.U., but where are they going to stand with any undergraduate group?

It must be obvious that Cornell cannot get up a dime toward the expenses of an Olympic trip for Rafer Johnson. In their inept way, the A.A.U. and Olympic Committee managed this. The college coaches who want to grab power don't even pretend that they can do the same.

Secessionist leaders are talking about setting up splinter organizations in track and field, basketball and gymnastics which would conduct rump championships in opposition to the A.A.U. meets and would pose as the national governing bodies in these sports. Penn State's Chick Werner, president of the Track Coaches, talks about running a federation meet on June 22 and 23, the dates of the National A.A.U. Championships. Implying that the coaches would hold undergraduate athletes, and any post-graduates they could influence, out of the A.A.U. carnival, he says the top pair in each event in both meets would have to be chosen for the dual meet with Russia in Palo Alto in July.

Precedent flatly contradicts this. Two American ice hockey teams went to Europe for the 1948 Winter Olympics, both claiming to be the official representative of the United States. One team was selected by the Hockey Committee of the United States Olympic Committee, the other by professional interests in Boston and New York. There was a sorry mess. The pros played, on a quasi-official basis, and the amateurs stood by matching a miserable performance complete with fist-fights and public booing.

A house divided is a disorderly house in any sport. A.A.U. experience in this field embraces three-quarters of a century. It was the A.A.U. that arranged the meet with Russia, and it is the A.A.U.'s responsibility to select and certify this country's representatives. The A.A.U. would not and should not abdicate this responsibility to appease a pack of howling malcontents.

It might be possible for the coaches to sabotage the A.A.U. championships and the meet with Russia by holding their boys out. It would be a flagrant abuse of authority for which they would be accountable to their colleges and to the kids whom they deprived of a chance for a national title and a shot at the Russians.

Loudly the N.C.A.A. politicos insist that this is not a power grab. In view of their record, methinks they doth protest too much. Once a rather loose fraternity concerned chiefly with schedule-making, this tong has been employing steamroller tactics for a decade to extend its influence in many directions.

It has arrogated to itself police powers in college sport, creating jobs for a whole force of gumshoes snooping into the affairs of large schools and small. Walter Byers and his gang have the gall to tell college presidents what is ethical and what is not. They have blandly assumed the right to sanction post-season football games, obviously the province of individual schools, and in this area they hand out franchises to promoters using college kids for private profit, and blacklist schools that participate in unsanctioned games.

On the pretext of undertaking a temporary inquiry into television's effect on the box office, they snatched away from the colleges the clear right to make their own TV deals and have perpetuated this authority through mob rule, with an implied threat to boycott any school that resists.

They still aren't smart enough to read, understand, interpret or correctly apply their own football rules, but just the same Jimmy Hoffa could learn a lot from these boys.

How the Russians Invented Beizbol

February 1962   New York

The Russian disclosure that Comrade Kasyi Stenglov, popularly supposed to be the inventor of beizbol, actually stole the game off the steppes of the Kremlin comes as no surprise to serious students of sports in America. The amazing thing is that the Russian people weren't told about it until the illustrated journal Nedelya broke the story this week.

Nedelya is published by the official newspaper Izvestia which in turn is edited by Nikita Khrushchev's son-in-law, Alexei Adzhubei, Pierre Salinger's buddy, who has been lolly-gagging around Pennsylvania Ave. lately digging up the dirt on our games from an old touch football star.

Presumably it was from this source the Nedelya learned about those crowds of 300,000 that often assembles in Yanqui Stadium to watch the Reds play the

Red Soxei in our corrupted version of the fine old Muscovite pastime of lapta.

There have been encouraging signs of a thaw around the edges of the cold war. A pup named Pushinka, the gift of Khrushchev himself, is a pet in the White House; Nikita's kinfolk have been fed hot dogs at the Bobby Kennedys'; Salinger's small son Steve played "The Star-Spangled Banner" on a fiddle while his sire took their Soviet guests boat-riding past Mount Vernon. There has even been talk of the Salingers and Adzhubeis swapping offspring for a few months.

Now that the campaign for better understanding has Nedelya advising its readers to "get acquainted with these interesting games (beizbol and golf)," the least we can do is reciprocate. Research into the history and nature of popular Russian pastimes has been undertaken, and the results are presented here as a public service.

Lapta, the ancestor of beizbol, derives its name from the Laptev Sea, an arm of the Arctic Ocean north of the Soviet Union between Taimyr Peninsula and the new Siberian islands. It was in the little town of Kupyrhgrad on the shore of this sea that lapta was invented in the summer of 1839.

The inventor was one Abnov Dublinsky, then a cadet in the Tsarist military academy at St. Petersburg, though at that time the city was known as Leningrad. After Dublinsky rose to the rank of general in the Crimean War and attained immortality as the inventor of lapta, the city where he was educated proudly changed its name to St. Petersburg, after the Florida town then serving as spring training base for the Yanquis, the greatest team in the game.

Tsar Nicholas II was assassinated in 1881. According to a Russian radio sportscaster named Ilya Sternov, who enjoyed a considerable vogue before television, as the ruler lay dying he called old Abnov to his bedside. "General Dublinsky," he whispered with his last mortal breath, "keep . . . lapta . . . alive!"

Lapta is played with a round stone, or lapis, and a flat stick on a field 29 meters square. With the fielders disposed in strategic positions, a player in the middle of the square throws the stone up for the man with the stick, while the thrower's teammates encourage him with merry cries of "stick it in his earovitch!"

On striking the stone with his stick (getting a beiz blau), the striker attempts to run around the boundaries of the square. If he can return to the starting point without being skulled by a thrown stone, he scores a point for his side.

After nine innings, survivors count up points and the team with the greater number wins.

Lapta players are popular heroes throughout the Soviet Union. Among the most famous and highly paid are Yogi Beria, Mikhail Mantell, Tyodor Vylyms, Stanislav Myusil, Vladimir Spahnoff and Vitei Fordnik.

Next to lapta, perhaps the most popular sport in the land is Russian roulette, a game of chance. Any number can play, but not for long.

The rules are simple and too widely known to require exposition here. The curious feature of this game is that it is the loser, rather than the winner, who achieves the most lasting renown.

To name just a few of the players whose names are still remembered: Leon Trotzky, Nicolai Lenin, Josef Stalin, Grigori Rasputin and Georgi Malenkov.

Recently chosen player-of-the-year for 1961 was Mikhailovitch Molotov.

Maris is Rude; Hornsby is Miffed

March 1962   St. Petersburg, Fla.

Rogers Hornsby of the Hall of Fame, mightiest of all National League hitters and the roughest right-handed bruiser in human history, was snooted by a .269 hitter the other day. He was miffed, and justifiably so. The refusal of Roger Maris to pose for a photograph with Hornsby was strictly bush.

Nevertheless, the importance of the incident, if it has any importance at all, has been widely exaggerated. For two consecutive days, a teapot tiff between two grown men has got bigger headlines than Algiers. The volume of space devoted this spring to Maris' pouts and sulks betrays a sorry sense of proportion and lends an element of justice to the outfielder's complaints about his treatment in the press.

Because he has not yet learned to live with fame, Maris has laid himself open to adverse criticism, and has got more than he deserves. He will suffer for it, probably is suffering for it now. If it teaches him a lesson, he can profit from the experience. If, through stubbornness, he becomes embittered, it can warp what should be a productive professional life.

This is not a defense of bad manners or mean pettiness. It is a plea for tolerance entered in the hope that the young man may get, and accept, a chance to grow up.

During last summer's tandem pursuit of Babe Ruth's ghost by Maris and Mickey Mantle, Maris was irked by a published comment from Hornsby, who said that in his judgment Maris was no great hitter and if either man was going to break Ruth's home run record it should by rights be Mantle, the better all-around player. Hornsby suggested that pitchers ought to "work" on Maris and give him fewer opportunities to pull the ball to right.

"How does he think they're pitching to me?" Maris demanded, perhaps not appreciating that he was getting a lot better stuff to hit than he would without Mantle batting behind him.

"No," he said here the other day when a photographer for United Press International brought Hornsby over for a picture, "all he does is run me down."

Hornsby was nettled by this rudeness but nobody has attached less importance to it than he. He was merely contemptuous.

"He couldn't carry my bats," said the man whose batting average for *five consecutive years* was .402. "Hell, my lifetime average (.358) is bigger than all his figures added together. I said he was a no-account hitter and I'd say it to his face right now." Then Hornsby forgot it, but nobody else has.

Though he has been employed by major league teams since 1957, Maris has had less than a year of education in a difficult school. It started late last summer when he was drawing close to Ruth's record. Such wild excitement surrounded him, he was badgered and hectored and harassed so that nobody who was around the Yankees could help feeling sympathetic toward a country kid who had never known anything like this before.

Sometimes he ran out of patience, as anybody would, but by and large he conducted himself creditably. This year he rejoined the Yankees as a famous man whose fame gives a false significance to almost everything he says or does. It wasn't he who changed over the winter. He still speaks his mind as he did in the past, not always tactfully. Sometimes he is bewildered, especially when some of his stoutest defenders of 1961 put the zing on him for saying the same sort of things they applauded last year.

His announcement that he would submit to no interviews this year may conceivably have been intended facetiously, for sometimes his efforts at humor are heavy-handed. However it was meant, it was interpreted as a symptom of swollen ego. At best, it was a mistake.

Oscar Fraley, of UPI, scolded him for it editorially, and after reading the column Maris had a shouting row with Fraley in the dugout. In the past he has sometimes beefed about something written by someone regularly assigned to the Yankees, and once he had blown off steam it was all forgotten. He gets on fine with the regulars covering the club.

This year, however, the scene with Fraley gets lumped together with other small things and contributes to "the changing image of Roger Maris, 1962." Hell, Fraley had a right to criticize him for a foolish statement and he had a right to holler if he didn't like what Oscar wrote. Nobody enjoys a good scrap more than Fraley.

Holding a grudge against Hornsby for an honest statement of opinion, that was something else. It was childish. It was bush. But it was no more than that, and Hornsby himself regarded it as nothing more.

Maris shouldn't be applauded for acting like a boor or a chump. Neither should he be pictured as one who burns down orphanages. Give him a little more time.

Outcries in Paret Case ... Ray Arcel

April 1962   Salisbury, N. C.

The pitiful case of Benny Paret moves each according to his nature. The habitually hysterical raise the scream of "legalized murder," and their number includes some who are equally quick to revile any fighter who, unlike Paret, quits under punishment. The politicians fulminate as politicians must, like that cluck in the South Carolina Legislature who wants a law requiring circular or 10-sided rings so a fighter can't be trapped in a corner.

Prodded perhaps by fear or maybe by conscience, Manny Alfaro, Paret's manager, gave a disgraceful performance trying to pin the blame on Ruby Goldstein, the referee. Nobody involved has any right to blame anybody else for a tragic accident, least of all a manager who gets his boy cruelly beaten by Gene Fullmer, then sends him back against a man who has already been knocked out.

To me boxing is a rough, dangerous and thrilling sport, the most basic and natural and uncomplicated of athletic competitions, and—at its best—one of the purest of art forms. Yet there is no quarrel here with those who sincerely regard it as a vicious business that should have no place in a civilized society.

They are wrong, of course, those who think boxing can be legislated out of existence. It has been tried a hundred times, but there were always men ready to fight for prizes on a barge or in a pasture lot or the back room of a saloon. It is hard to believe that a nation bereft of such men would be the stronger or better for it.

Still, if a man honestly feels that boxing should be abolished, he has every right to cite the Paret case in support of his position. The quarrel here is with the part-time bleeding-hearts, the professional sob-sisters of press and politics and radio who seize these opportunities to

159

parade their own nobility, demonstrate their eloquence, and incidentally stir the emotions of a few readers, voters or listeners.

Some of the fakers now sobbing publicly over Paret have waxed ecstatic over a Ray Robinson or Joe Louis. It must be comforting to have it both ways.

Sometimes it seems there are more frauds outside boxing than in it. At least, the professionals are realists who recognize the game for the rough business it is, and accept the stern code which demands that a beaten man go on fighting as long as he is able to stay on his feet.

This doesn't mean that all card-carrying members of the fight mob are cut to the Hollywood-and-pulp-fiction pattern—scheming, selfish, dishonest mercenaries devoid of all decent feeling. A gentleman like Ray Arcel, the great trainer, can spend a lifetime in the dodge without dishonor, but he must subscribe to the code.

One night Ray was in the corner of a boy pacifist whose innate repugnance of violence was aggravated by the shots his adversary kept bouncing off his chin. Between rounds the boy expressed a devout wish to be elsewhere.

"Hang in there," Ray said. "He's as tired as you are."

Reluctantly the young man returned to the conflict. With a most unneighborly scowl his opponent advanced and the boy backed off warily, into his own corner.

"Ray," he said from behind a half clenched glove, "throw in the towel, will ya?"

"Just keep punching," Ray said. "You're all right."

The tiger fled backward, buffeted and breathless. His knees were wobbly but he managed to stay up for a full circuit of the ring.

"Please, Ray," he gasped, passing his corner, "throw in the towel now."

"Box him," Ray called after him. "Stick him and move."

The pursuit race continued for another dizzying lap.

"Ray," the hero begged, "please throw in the towel. I won't be around again."

It should not be inferred that Arcel is impervious to punishment or in any degree lacking in compassion.

Among the hundreds of fighters he has handled, a special favorite was the gallant Jackie Kid Berg, whom he called by a pet name, Yitzel.

Crouching in Berg's corner one night, Ray winced and shuddered in vicarious pain as a ferocious body-puncher poured lefts and rights into Jackie's middle. Sometimes the whistling gloves seemed to disappear altogether, bringing a gasp from Berg and a groan from his handler. Still up and fighting back when the round ended, Jackie did an about-face at the bell and marched back to his corner.

"Yitzel!" Ray said shakily, "how do you feel?"

"Fine, thank you," the Kid said. "And you?"

Yogi's 2,000th Game—Guess Who Win It

June 1962   New York

When Yogi Berra shuffled up to the plate, the game stopped. Jim Honochick, the umpire, called for the ball from Dick Hall, the Baltimore pitcher, handed it to Berra and produced a new one. Yogi kept the first and lost the second in the right field seats. In his 2,000th game with the Yankees, his home run was the winning blow.

Two thousand games earlier was the first half of a double-header on Sunday, Sept. 22, 1946. Berra caught nine innings against the Philadelphia Athletics and no-body stole on him. He whacked little Jesse Flores for a home run and a single and drove in two runs as the third-place Yankees won, 4-3, for Johnny Neun, the manager pro tem. This was the Yankee batting order that day:

George Stirnweiss, 2b; Tommy Henrich, 1b; Bobby Brown, ss; Joe DiMaggio, cf; Charley Keller, lf; Bill Johnson, 3b; Johnny Lindell, rf; Berra, and Spud Chandler, p. "Of considerable interest," wrote Harold Rosenthal in The Herald Tribune, "was the appearance of several recent Yankee acquisitions. Bobby Brown, Newark's hard-hitting shortstop, made his debut as did Larry Berra, Newark catcher." The next day a "likely looking lad" named Vic Raschi pitched and won his first game for the Yankees.

No need to ask where they all are now. Where was Dick Hall, the Baltimore pitcher, in September, 1946? He was approaching his 16th birthday in St. Louis. And Jim Honochick? He was a rookie umpire in the Eastern Shore League, having played until midsummer as an outfielder for Baltimore in the International League.

In terms of service to an organization, just what do 2,000 games mean? Well, if Johnny Neun, Bucky Harris, Casey Stengel and Ralph Houk had decided, in their infinite wisdom, to play Yogi at one position all the time, he would by last year have caught more games than any other man who ever wore the tools of ignorance. Because he was employed also as an outfielder, third baseman and first baseman, he leaves the lifetime catching record to Al Lopez, with 1,910 games.

In the 15 seasons completed since 1946, the Yankees have won 12 pennants and nine world championships, finished second once and third twice. They have had stars of the first magnitude through those years, DiMaggio and Keller and Henrich, Phil Rizzuto and Mickey Mantle and Roger Maris, Allie Reynolds and Ed Lopat and Whitey Ford.

One constant factor has remained while the others came and went. One was there before Stengel and is there now that Stengel is gone. Nobody can say the Yankees

would not have won all those championships without
Berra, but the simple fact is that he was there helping
with everyone, and playing a huge part in the winning.

It is not possible to exaggerate his importance. He
has been the keystone, the binder, the adhesive element
that has held this team together when everything else
changed.

Early in 1947 a visitor was sitting on the Yankees'
bench between Bucky Harris and Al Schacht. Berra
slouched by on his way to the water cooler. Bucky
nudged the visitor and, speaking behind a hand, muttered
into his left ear, "A character." At the same moment
there was a nudge from the right. "A character,"
Schacht murmured into that ear.

Actually, Yogi was not yet either a character or a
catcher, officially. His name was Larry Berra, not Yogi.
Harris was using him as an outfielder and his defensive
talents reflected no high polish, either out there or behind the plate.

Later Bill Dickey was to take him in hand to smooth
the rough spots from his technique. "Bill is learning me
his experiences," Yogi said. That helped make him a
character, and Dickey helped make him a catcher.

To say merely that he became a great one is to under-
play his value to the team. In spite of his curious construction, he moved with astonishing agility around the
plate. He learned the hitters and he never forgot anything he learned. He could, and still can, con and cosset
and calm a harried pitcher who would spit in the manager's eye if he were to walk out. His throwing and running were exceptional, and with a stick in his paws he
is pure poetry.

"And," Casey used to say, "he knows what they're
thinkin' in the front office."

At first he was so eager to hit that he swung at pitches
Wilt Chamberlain couldn't reach. Somebody, memory
suggests Birdie Tebbetts, remarked that it would be easy
to run Yogi out of the league. "Walk him intentionally
four times in a row," he said, "and he'd quit baseball."
Today they say that when Yogi discards a bat which he
has squeezed dry of hits, it is marked only in a single

spot, the fat part which that lovely swing of his brings around to meet the ball again and again.

Over 16 years Yogi accepted all the hazards and suffered all the catcher's occupational ills—the split fingers and cracked knuckles, the sprains and spavins and bruises. Yet summer after summer he hung in there doing the work of two, sometimes catching double-headers when he was hot with fever or aching with 'flu, catching even while he nursed, of all things, an allergy to the leather mitt.

The Yankees have had many great ones, but no other quite like this one. "Why," the late Rud Rennie protested the first time he saw this rookie up from Newark, "he doesn't even look like a Yankee." Perhaps he didn't then. Today if somebody were to ask what a Yankee looked like, whose image would come to mind?

World Series Golf: Palmer, Player, Nicklaus

August 1962   New York

The golden boy of golf, Arnold Palmer, watched an 18-foot putt curl into the cup on Akron's Firestone course, straightened, and made his polite thank you's for another $9,000. First money in a routine tournament called the American Classic brought his prizes for the year to a gaudy $80,198.

Three weeks hence while the peons of professional golf are at Denver competing for fragments of a $30,-000 pot, Palmer, Gary Player and Jack Nicklaus will return to the same course to cut up $75,000 three ways. More power, and money, to the three of them. They have earned their rewards on merit. When Palmer becomes the first golfer to pocket more than $100,000 on prizes in a single year, it can be truly said that it couldn't happen to a nicer guy.

Yet in permitting it to happen this way, the leadership of the Professional Golfers' Association has repudiated its own rule book, broken faith with its membership and their sponsors, stultified and disqualified themselves. The P.G.A. sanction of a glorified exhibition called the "World Series" of golf is a flagrant reversal of precedent. The fact that the same men established the precedent by a series of contradictory injustices only compounds their fault.

Dictatorial though its official actions sometimes are, the P.G.A. does not have authority to insist on any member's participation in any tournament. The by-laws recognize, however, that unless sponsors have some assurance of getting a good box office attraction, they can't afford big prize money. So it is provided that the stars—the top money-earners and winners of specified tournaments—may not take part in any competition whose dates conflict with those of a P.G.A.-approved event.

Applying this rule last year, the brass forbade Palmer, Player and Canada's Stan Leonard to represent their countries in the Canada Cup and International Championship in Puerto Rico because the Memphis Open would be on at the same time.

Considering that the Canada Cup matches involve only two players from any country, it was a dog-in-the-manger attitude which the Memphis promotors took, and the P.G.A. bosses didn't distinguish themselves, either. Privately they sneer at the Canada Cup as "nothing but an exhibition" because it is an invitational event with the P.G.A. having no voice in selecting the field. But the rule on conflicting tournaments doesn't apply to exhibitions, so in this instance the brass recognized the Canada Cup as bona fide competition.

Sam Snead, invited as United States representative with Palmer, hadn't won enough to make the "star" category, so he was allowed to go to Puerto Rico, where he and Jimmy Demarest won.

Later in the summer, Snead entered a pro-amateur event in Cincinnati instead of an approved tournament in Portland, Ore. He hadn't been in the "star" group at Canada Cup time and he hadn't won anything in between, but now the P.G.A. heads reversed themselves, slapping him with a fine and suspension.

To give their action the appearance of calculated malice, they made the penalty retroactive by dropping Snead from the Ryder Cup team, an honor he had striven for and won much earlier.

These, then, were the admirable precedents: Snead could play in conflict with the Memphis Open but Palmer, Player and Leonard couldn't; however, Sam could not play in conflict with the Portland event, and he couldn't play in the Ryder Cup matches at all.

So now sponsors dug up $75,000 and said how about letting Palmer, Player and Nicklaus make this television show in conflict with the Denver Open. Peachy, said the P.G.A. brainbund.

Palmer is the Masters' and British Open champion, Nicklaus owns the U. S. Open title and Player the American P.G.A. Having put up $30,000, the Denver sponsors lose the three biggest box office names in the game, plus Bob Rosburg who will do the TV commentary from Akron.

The official explanation is that the Akron show is just an exhibition. This is at least partly true, but to say so officially is to slug the promoters, who are knocking themselves out to build it up as a genuine world championship. Tying on the "exhibition" tag helps spread the rumor—hotly denied by the promoters—that the three players, all under the same management, will take a flat $25,000 each instead of competing for $50,000 in first money, $15,000 for second and $10,000 for third.

Recently Lou Strong, P.G.A. president, was asked how much money his organization was getting from the Akron promotion.

"I do not care to answer that question," he said.

A Not-so-Typical Day at the Races

August 1962   Saratoga Springs

When the field broke in the fifth race, a dark gelding named Exhibit A dashed off in front as though he could read the tote board, where he was a smashing favorite

166

at 1-to-3. Just off the pace was Otsego, a 3-year-old owned by Mrs. Stephen C. Clark, jr., of Cooperstown, which had raced five times and broken his maiden the last time out. He was 15-to-1 on the board.

This was a race called the Promise, a-mile-and-five-eights over hurdles, with $12,500-added. The rider on Otsego was Jimmy Murphy, a small man in his upper 30s who has been riding jumpers trained by Sidney Watters, jr., about as long as anybody can remember.

Jimmy Murphy hasn't been the luckiest man on the race track. They say he has brittle bones, which isn't ideal equipment for a rider of jump races. He's had his collarbone broken something like 17 times. In the first week at Saratoga last August he went down with a smash that meant a longish stretch in hospital with a broken leg.

He keeps getting up and riding, though. If they grow 'em brittle in Ligonier, Pa., they don't short-change 'em on courage. He has kept busy this year, and stands second to Pat Smithwick in the national rankings, with 12 winners, 12 seconds and 8 thirds in 55 races.

Up front on Exhibit A, Willard Thompson had two fistfuls of running horse. The favorite drew off easily with his rider sitting still—two lengths, three, five. Murphy had Otsego third behind Kantikoy, then second, then third again.

From the stands, 13,363 watched with pleasure. It was one of the finest days of the meeting, bright and mild, and the green turf was firm. Horse fans like hurdle races, where the jumps aren't frightening like the steeplechase fences but just high enough to add a fillip of excitement to the pretty spectacle.

Eight of the nine jumps went off smoothly. Coming around the last turn, Thompson let his mount out a notch and Exhibit A went to the last barrier leading his field by six big lengths. He was over and reaching out for the last stretch of flat when Murphy sent his tiring mount into the fence.

When a horse is tired, young riders are told, don't let him loaf into a jump unless you enjoy being hurt. Send him at it as hard as he'll go. Murphy did. For an instant

167

horse and rider seemed to hang in midair. Then both came down head first.

The horse came down on his head, somersaulted, gave two or three convulsive kicks and lay still. Murphy, thrown just ahead, was a limp little figure in white as the field jumped clear. From the grandstand area a girl started running, his wife.

Ambulance, outriders, Dr. John A. Esposito, Pinkertons and assistant starters were moving before the favorite reached the wire, 12 lengths ahead of the 35-to-1 Scuderia, who came on from far back under a drive by Tommy Burns, a fugitive from the flats.

Murphy was lifted on a stretcher and the ambulance cut across the infield bound directly for the hospital. The doctor rode with him. Steve Clark, who had joined the group, bent over his horse. Otsego was dead, his neck was broken. A wooden screen was set up, and behind it the horse was dragged into a van.

"The result of the fifth race is official," Fred Capossela said over the public address system. "The winner, Exhibit A—" The tote flashed the shortest price of the meeting, $2.70, but there were cries for the return on Scuderia, $14.30 for place.

A horse was dead, a rider unconscious. The horse players scanned their form sheets on the sixth race. In the press box, a phone wire was opened to the hospital.

Murphy, the first report said, had regained consciousness and his only visible injury was a laceration on the forehead. A little later, lacerations of face, arms and hands were reported. Finally came word of a mild concussion. The patient would remain overnight for observation. For jumping horse riders, that's the name of the game.

"We are happy to report," Capossela told the crowd, "that jockey James Murphy is not seriously injured." There was quite a polite little patter of applause.

Greed and Godliness in the Majors

Two factors guide the men who draw up plane schedules in major league baseball—greed and godliness. Night
games are taboo on Sundays because this is a sacred
time reserved by the righteous for cook-outs, Ed Sullivan
and drinking whiskey. (In their simple piety, the club
owners have overlooked the fact that Friday is the holy
day in some faiths and Saturday in others.) Outside of
desecrating the Christian Sabbath by turning on flood-
lights, anything goes if it's profitable.

The Pittsburgh Pirates knew this when they threatened
a strike to avoid day and night games in St. Louis Saturday with a double-header yesterday afternoon. There is
nothing in the rules to support them, and they backed
down.

Nevertheless, they were dead right to object, and
should have stuck to their position. There would have
been no sympathy for the bosses.

The issue arose when rain washed out Friday night's
game in the third inning. Because this was the season's
last series with the Cardinals, the Pirates offered to play
off the postponed game as part of a Saturday afternoon
double-header or this afternoon or evening, today being
open for both teams. However, for two Saturday afternoon
games, only one admission could be charged.

Baseball owners have moral scruples against taking
any man's dollar when there is a chance to take a dollar
and a quarter. They insisted on their plan to offer two
games for the price of two. They drew 15,369 customers
Saturday afternoon and 8,959 Saturday night.

All it cost the players was their rights and their sleep.
For a regular double-header it is customary to report
for work about 11 a.m. Saturday's games consumed four
hours, 18 minutes. Starting at 1:30 p.m. with a half-

hour intermission, the players could have got to the showers a little after 6 p.m.

Instead they remained at the park all day without a square meal, got to the hotel for a sandwich and beer around midnight, and may have made the sack by 3 a.m.

Assuming that they were now relaxed and at peace, they could count on something like six hours' rest, except for those with religious scruples like their bosses'. They'd be up earlier for church.

Some of the Pirates had the dreamy notion that there was some sort of rule against a night game on the eve of a double-header. They were told it didn't apply on their last visit to a town. Somebody ought to tell them no schedule rules apply when the owners choose to ignore them.

While revolt was simmering in St. Louis, the Yankees were enjoying a carefree excursion of their own. After three hard games in Los Angeles, two at night and a 13-inning defeat Thursday afternoon, they had an all-night flight to Baltimore for a twi-night double-header starting at 6 p.m. Friday.

They managed to lose twice before midnight. Two or three hours later, they were racked out with nothing to bother their pretty heads about except a day-and-night double-header Saturday.

That meant another working day of noon to midnight, but Sunday would be a cinch. Just one lousy afternoon game, then home without a thing to do until the Indians come calling tonight.

Probably playing ball for a living beats opening oysters, but the advantages aren't what they were. Nobody can curb the owners' avarice except the players and the players have themselves to blame for some of their discomforts, at least.

There used to be a rule against get-away games at night.

In exchange for the owners' sanction of that lamentable second All-Star game to swell the Pension Fund, the players waived this restriction, which was never strictly enforced, anyhow. Now they want the rule reinstated and observed, but they don't want to give up that additional All-Star loot.

They also want relief in the form of a shortened schedule of 153 games, one fewer than they played when they had eight-club leagues. This would mean 17-game series; an American League owner who used to have the Yankees dragging customers to his park 11 times a year would have them in nine times one season, and eight the next.

It is a shocking proposal to put to any owner. What do they think he's in this game for—sport?

Bo Belinsky ... and the Tale of an Idle Rumor

September 1962   New York

Declaring Kansas City off limits for Bo Belinsky, Ford Frick said sternly that "gentlemen's agreements are not permitted" in baseball. Not permitted, for Pete's sake? If the words mean what Webster thought they did, they're not possible.

For the benefit of any clients who've been living in caves lately without daily news delivery, perhaps it should be explained that this case broke open with the publication of a story that Belinsky, the leftwing Angel who pitched a no-hitter in the spring, would be shipped to the Athletics after this season as the second and last installment on Dan Osinski, the relief pitcher purchased by Los Angeles from the Kansas City chain in July.

There is nothing unusual or improper about swapping a player for a down payment plus a man "to be selected later," but those words have to mean what they say. If the clubs involved agree privately at the time of the deal on the identity of the man to be delivered later, it can be illegal for several reasons.

One reason is that Los Angeles bought Osinski after the deadline for exchanging big league players, except through waivers. They tried but couldn't get waivers on Belinsky, who was claimed by Washington. Thus, agreeing to hang on to Bo for the rest of the season and then send him to Kansas City would be circumventing the waiver rules.

There is a more important reason for the rule against "gentlemen's agreements." If a secret deal has been made for a player, chances are he'll hear about it, as Belinsky did. Theoretically, if he knows he's going to be playing for Kansas City next year, he might not be disposed to treat the A's harshly when he pitches against them this year.

Actually, he'd probably bear down all the harder, because he'd want to make the biggest possible impression on the men who'll be talking contract with him next winter. But the public might suspect his motives, especially if he got shellacked.

"What the hell," the cynical would say, "he knows he's going to be one of the family next season. He dumped this one for his future employer."

It is Ford Frick's job as commissioner to make sure that baseball avoids the appearance of evil, not just evil itself. This is why he had no choice, once the story broke, but to forbid the transfer of Belinsky to Kansas City at any time in the foreseeable future.

In a way it's too bad. The mouthy pool player from Trenton, N.J., turned Hollywood boulevardier, is less than one year removed from the bush. He and the Kansas City owner, Charles O. Finley, might have found much in common.

Naturally, everybody concerned denied for publication that a sub rosa deal had been made. Chances are everybody denied it to Frick, too, this being protocol. However, the commissioner needed no firm evidence to take action. He had to act as soon as the story became common currency.

He knows, of course, that "gentlemen's agreements" are made all the time, and that often the "gentlemen" get by with them. Probably he remembered a case that came up when he was president of the National League and Kenesaw Mountain Landis was commissioner.

Larry MacPhail, then running the Brooklyn Dodgers, coveted Rube Melton, a minor league pitcher eligible for the draft. It seemed certain, though, that some team lower in the league than Brooklyn would grab Melton before MacPhail's turn came.

It became common gossip that MacPhail made a proposition to Gerry Nugent, whose last-place Phillies had first call in the draft but couldn't afford the price.

"You claim Melton," Larry was supposed to have said, "and I'll buy him from you for twice the draft price."

Sure enough, at the October draft meeting the Phillies did select the Rube. A hoarse stage whisper of triumph was heard around the table: "We got him! We got him!" Everybody recognized the voice. And sure enough, a month or so later the Phils announced sale of Melton to Brooklyn.

During the December meetings in Chicago, Landis called in MacPhail, Nugent and their managers. To anybody unacquainted with the judge's theatrical proclivities, it could have seemed an accident that the transom was left open between the commissioner's office and the foyer where the press waited.

The press got an earful. MacPhail howled implications at Leslie O'Connor, Landis' gumshoe. O'Connor bawled accusations at MacPhail. The judge shouted both down. At length they all emerged and Landis announced, "The sale of pitcher Melton's contract is disallowed."

Gerry Nugent was approached for a statement. Instead of turning a quick profit, he now had to scrape up the draft price somewhere for a pitcher he never meant to claim. Though deeply saddened, he obliged with a masterful statement.

"It all goes to show," he said, "what an idle rumor can do."

The Vigilantes

October 1962   San Francisco

In the last World Series game, Mickey Mantle added 34 points to his batting average. One single in three chances brought him to .120. He also walked once, whereupon Jack Sanford picked him off first base with admirable celerity.

Nothing could illustrate better the quality of pitching which lent such rich, crunchy goodness to the rounders tournament. The curtain scene, gripping though it was, may have lacked a little of the wild and implausible melodrama that closed the 1960 Series in Pittsburgh, but this was finer baseball and cleaner theater throughout. Stretched out over seven games and 13 days, it had everything but continuity.

Nevertheless, the Vigilantes were riding the unlittered streets yesterday, thirsting for Whitey Lockman's blood. It's hard to blame the natives. They never had a World Series before and hardly expected to see this one. Having come to believe in miracles, they would have been crushed if their demi-gods had got clobbered in the final match; to have the decision slip down the drain, 1-0, enraged them.

Even though allowances are made, however, the oral and printed abuse of Lockman is slightly outrageous. The second guess is almost always unfair because it is a judgment made at leisure and influenced by subsequent developments which could not be foreseen at the instant

174

of the first guess. In this case it's doubly scandalous because Lockman was right and his critics are downright wrong-headed.

The First Guess

The issue, of course, was whether the Giants' coach at third base should have let Matty Alou try to score the tying run from first base on Willie Mays' double to right with two out in the ninth inning. The Yankees played the ball cleanly, and it says here the odds were 10 to 1 against Alou. However, even with a 50-50 chance, Lockman would have been foolish to send Alou in.

When your team is only one putout this side of extinction, you simply must not run any considerable risk of giving away that last out. If the score were tied and Alou represented the winning run, the gamble could be justified, for the Giants would still be entitled to another turn at bat. That was the situation in 1946 when Country Slaughter ran home from first to win the championship for the Cardinals.

In this case, Willie McCovey was coming to bat. He is a lefthanded batter. On his last turn against the right-handed Ralph Terry, he had ripped a monstrous triple into centerfield for one of San Francisco's four hits.

When he tore into Terry's first pitch with Mays on second and Alou on third, Lockman's decision looked good. McCovey hit that pitch far over the fence, but the wind pushed it foul. He hit the next pitch even better. Luck alone steered it straight into Bobby Richardson's glove instead of a yard to right or left for the ball game.

Manager Ralph Terry

Had that drive gone safe, Lockman would be immortalized as the Sage of San Francisco and Ralph Houk would be getting chewed out for not ordering an intentional base on balls for McCovey. That would have been

175

unfair, too, for it was Terry who made the decision to pitch to the big guy.

Before the commotion raised by Mays' hit had subsided, the Yankee manager was on the mound consulting his pitcher. First base was open, and putting a runner on would cost the Yankees nothing because the game and Series would end if Mays scored from second.

Orlando Cepeda, a righthanded hitter, would be up behind McCovey. Though Cepeda had been a terror in the sixth game when he got a double and two singles, they were his only hits of the Series and he had been in a wretched slump for weeks. Against Terry in this game, he had struck out twice and popped up.

"I'd rather pitch to McCovey," Terry said.

"You're pitching the game," Houk told him. "Go ahead."

As Yogi Berra would say in his Left Bank French, Terry had *raison*. With the bases filled, he would have to use extreme caution with Cepeda. If he got behind him in the count, he would have to come in with good pitches, suited to Orlando's educated taste.

Willie For President

So Terry aimed for McCovey's fists—"jamming him" is the trade term. McCovey hit where he was supposed to hit, and the Yankees had their 20th championship in 40 years. When you consider that over most of those years, there were 15 other clubs after the same prize, then 17 and now 19 others, the record makes the Yankees look a mite hoggish. And slightly good.

Incidentally, there'll always be a Willie Mays. Almost invariably after a player had made a noteworthy home run, such as Chuck Hiller's blow with the bases filled in the fourth game, he says, "I was just trying to meet the pitch for a single."

After slicing his double, Willie was asked whether he'd been deliberately aiming for rightfield.

"No," he said, "I was only trying to hit it out of the park."

176

Index

179

183